U. S. WAR AIMS

U. S. WAR AIMS

By

WALTER LIPPMANN

AN ATLANTIC MONTHLY PRESS BOOK

LITTLE, BROWN AND COMPANY · BOSTON

1944

ATLANTIC—LITTLE, BROWN BOOKS
ARE PUBLISHED BY
LITTLE, BROWN AND COMPANY
IN ASSOCIATION WITH
THE ATLANTIC MONTHLY PRESS

To the Memory of
WILLIAM ALLEN WHITE

ACKNOWLEDGMENTS

As MY BOOK *U. S. Foreign Policy* was going to press in the spring of 1943, William Allen White, who had read the manuscript, called me on the telephone urging me to add another chapter showing how the wartime alliance of the four great powers could become the means to a good and lasting peace. I had to tell him that I could not write the chapter because the outcome of the war was still too uncertain, that until we began to see more clearly not only that the war would be won but at least in its grand outlines how it would be won, what anyone said about the settlement could be little more than guessing and hoping. Since then much has happened and great decisions have been made. This book is, I like to think, the chapter which William Allen White asked for, and I have dedicated it to his memory.

I am deeply in debt to Edward Weeks, the editor of the *Atlantic Monthly*. He has edited this book, and without his encouragement, his constant guidance, and his criticism, I do not see how it could have been completed.

In the research for the materials, in the ordering and preparation of the text, and in clarifying the argument, I have worked closely with Miss Frances Van Schaick, and I acknowledge gratefully her support and her help.

For working long hours on the many drafts of the manuscript, I wish to thank Miss Janet Bubier.

Since the book deals with current and future questions of high policy in this country and others, I cannot for obvious reasons make specific acknowledgments to the men now in official life whom I have consulted. But I can speak of certain of my friends, Lewis W. Douglas, Colonel David W. Wainhouse, Raymond Gram Swing, André Géraud ("Pertinax"), and the late Philip Kerr, Marquess of Lothian.

W. L.

Washington, D. C.
May 1944

CONTENTS

PART TWO

The Great Communities

PART THREE

The Settlement with the Enemy

PART FOUR

A Long Peace or the Third World War

PART FIVE

On the Formation of a Universal Society

U. S. WAR AIMS

CHAPTER I

INTRODUCTION

"It is for us the living, rather, to be dedicated here to
the unfinished work which they who fought here have
thus far so nobly advanced." — *The Gettysburg Address*

THE TIME has come and the way is clear to define our
war aims.

We could not have done this last year, much less at
the time when war was declared. For the decision to
resist when we were challenged is not what anyone
means by a war aim. That was a decision to stop our
enemies from achieving their war aims. On the day after
Pearl Harbor the Congress could say only that a state of
war existed and that it must be brought to a "successful
termination." The President, who has the constitutional
duty of deciding when hostilities shall end, has said they
will end when our principal enemies surrender unconditionally. This is not a statement of war aims but of our
purpose to wage war until the armed forces of Japan and
Germany can no longer oppose us. General principles
like those set down in the Atlantic Charter and the Four
Freedoms are not what we mean by war aims. They are
stars by which we can set our course. But it is the rough
and broken country immediately ahead through which

we have to make our way. It is to this task that true war aims, as I conceive them, must be addressed.

When we have answered the question of how, as the saying goes, the civilians can win the peace when the soldiers have won the war, we shall have defined our war aims. This question could not be answered by anyone in 1941 and 1942. For while we were determined to win the war, no one could foresee how it would be won. In December 1941 we did not know whether we could hold Hawaii, Alaska, and Australia. We did not know whether or how we could ever reach China before she was completely conquered. Even in 1942 we did not know but that Germany would break through the Middle East and Japan through India, but that they would join hands in the Indian Ocean, and isolate China altogether. . . . We did not know that Russia could repel the German invasion, much less did we imagine that within two years the Red Army would be in Poland, Romania, and Czechoslovakia.

How could we have formulated terms for Japan, not knowing what would become of China, Russia, Britain, in the Far East? Or terms for Germany, even supposing Great Britain and the United States could have defeated her, if Russia had been knocked out of the war in 1941 as she was in 1914? Until the battles of Midway, Stalingrad, Guadalcanal, El Alamein, and Tunisia had been fought and won, no responsible approach could be made to our war aims.

Only now in the spring of 1944 can we see the outcome of the war clearly enough to define our true war aims. I think we shall not be deceiving ourselves when we believe that a great and long peace is within our reach, and that we face an opportunity unlike any that has presented itself for centuries. First we must make certain that this war cannot be renewed by our present enemies, and that our allies will not become our future enemies. Then we can broaden the peace. But the first steps towards peace are certain to be the critical ones; a false turn down the wrong road can commit us to disasters even worse than those we have surmounted. Therefore, we must be sure-footed at the beginning. We must spare ourselves no trouble in endeavoring to judge correctly what is necessary and what is possible, what is feasible that is desirable, where are the pitfalls and where the highroad.

How then can the civilians win the peace when the soldiers have won the war? The question can now be answered, not to be sure in full detail, but sufficiently so that we may see where we are going and what we should do. The answer is that the civilians who shape the peace must first keep, and then develop, the gains which have been achieved by the stupendous sacrifice and effort of the war. This is the essence of the matter. This is what Lincoln said when he told his countrymen to dedicate themselves to the *unfinished work* which those who fight have *thus far so nobly advanced*.

We shall not squander the victory, as we did twenty-five years ago, if we hold fast to this simple idea: that the fundamental task of diplomats and public men is to conserve what is being accomplished by the war. No one can sit in his study or at a conference table and invent the plan of a workable peace. No one can invent a tree: he can nurse it, prune it, check the pests that would devour it; he can brace it against the storms. The peace will not be made after the fighting stops. It is being made, and, in great substance, it is already made. The only peace we can have is this one, the one now being wrought by waging the war, and we are presumptuous if we think that we can ignore this peace and make a different one.

When our enemies cry quits, we shall have in our possession the shape and structure of the peace. We do not have to build it. It has been built by heroic deeds and prodigious labor. We have to see that we do not tear it down. Then that we tend it and keep it standing. Then that we make it stronger. Then that we begin to improve it. If the survivors realize what has been wrought, they will find that they are inheriting a great peace which men have put together with their blood, their sweat, and their tears, and that this peace can endure if we are faithful to its essence and to its promise.

This book is intended to be a report which begins with why we are at war and goes on to show how the way we have waged the war has shaped the peace that we must conserve and perfect. When we know why in truth we are fighting, how in fact we have fought, what in reality we have won, we shall know how to define our war aims.

PART ONE

The Irreconcilable Conflicts

CHAPTER II

THE JAPANESE WAR

WE SHALL fix our attention on those critical facts and events which made the conflict with Japan and with Germany irreconcilable. I must emphasize the word *irreconcilable* because every country has disputes. But only those disputes are irreconcilable where the interest at stake is so vital to both countries that they would rather fight than give way.

1. The Issue at Pearl Harbor

We may begin by asking how we have come to be at war with Japan. It is true that Japan attacked Pearl Harbor on December 7, 1941, and that then we had no choice. But we cannot leave it at that. For the Japanese would not have attacked Pearl Harbor if we had accepted the terms they offered us. They did not attack Pearl Harbor for the sake of sinking our Pacific fleet. They tried to sink our Pacific fleet because we were opposing them on matters that they were determined to carry through.[1]

[1] Cf. *Papers Relating to the Foreign Relations of the United States. Japan: 1931–1941.* U. S. Government Printing Office, Washington, 1943.

There is no mystery about what these were. Japan was committed to the conquest of China. Japan was also planning and preparing the conquest of the East Indies, the Philippines, Malaya, and Indo-China. She was certainly contemplating an attack on the Soviet Union. But the irrevocable commitment was to conquer China: the rest, though there is no doubt that it was intended, was not an absolute and immediate commitment. The Japanese were willing to negotiate, to compromise, and at least to postpone, their demands outside of China.[2] There was the irreconcilable issue. When the United States refused finally to assent to the conquest of China, and to desist from opposing Japan in China, Japan went to war.

The Emperor's rescript declaring war against the United States and Britain [3] stated that war

> has been truly unavoidable [*because* the Chinese] regime which has survived at Chungking, relying upon American and British protection, still continues its fratricidal opposition

to the Nanking regime which accepts Japanese rule in occupied China. The Emperor went on to say that the United States and Britain,

[2] The Japanese offer of November 20, 1941.

[3] Japan declared war on December 7, 1941, at 4 P.M. E.S.T.; the attack on Pearl Harbor began at 1:20 P.M. E.S.T. The text is from the London *Times* translation. Cf. Leland M. Goodrich, *Documents on American Foreign Relations.* World Peace Foundation, Boston, 1942. Vol. IV, p. 115.

inducing other countries to follow suit, increased military preparations on all sides of our empire to challenge us. They have obstructed by every means our peaceful commerce, and finally have resorted to the direct severance of economic relations, menacing gravely the existence of our empire.

The statements are true. We did support the Chinese regime at Chungking. We encouraged it and helped it wage war against the Japanese invaders and their Chinese puppet government. We did induce Britain and the Netherlands to join us in preparing for war with Japan. We did sever economic relations, and our purpose was to impair the military power of the Japanese Empire.

On November 26, 1941, eleven days before Pearl Harbor, Secretary Hull gave the Japanese Ambassador the outline of an agreement to preserve the peace: it stipulated that

the Government of Japan will withdraw all military, naval, air and police forces from China and from Indo-China.[4]

Mr. Hull's memorandum was the American reply to the Japanese proposal (November 20) which contained no offer to evacuate China, and in fact demanded that the United States "refrain" from intervening in the relations between Japan and China.[5] This was the irreconcilable issue. On the American demand that Japan evacuate

[4] *Foreign Relations of the United States. Japan: 1931–1941.* Vol. II, p. 769.
[5] *Ibid.*, p. 755.

China and the Japanese demand that the United States abandon China, the final negotiations broke down.[6] Mr. Kurusu told Mr. Hull that our position would be interpreted in Tokyo "as tantamount to meaning the end." [7] Three days later Mr. Hull told the British Ambassador that

> the diplomatic part of our relations with Japan was virtually over and that the matter will now go to the officials of the Army and Navy.[8]

A week later the Japanese attacked Pearl Harbor.

2. America the Champion of China

The question, then, is why and how the United States, rather than assent to the conquest of China, chose to

[6] "Hope of concluding any arrangement, however, became slender indeed in the light of clear indication given by the Japanese authorities that they had no intention of desisting from the menace which they were creating to the United States, to the British Empire, to the Netherlands East Indies, to Thailand, and to China, by the substantial increasing of their armed forces in Indochina and in adjacent waters. In view of that growing menace, of the continuation of the hostilities in China, of the mobilization of Japanese forces in Manchuria, and of the fact that the Japanese proposal of November 20 offered, as outlined above, no basis for a practical and reassuring settlement, it was obvious that the chance of meeting the crisis by measures of diplomacy had practically vanished." (*Ibid.*, pp. 370–371.)

[7] *Ibid.*, p. 766.

[8] *Peace and War. United States Foreign Policy 1931–1941*. U. S. Government Printing Office, Washington, 1943, p. 816.

accept the Japanese challenge. The record shows that the American nation reached this momentous decision gradually, reluctantly, but with increasing unanimity and finality, over a period of about forty years. The remarkable thing about the record of these forty years is the constancy with which the United States government has stood for the integrity of Chinese territory.

The first President to take this position was McKinley: in 1900 his Secretary of State, John Hay, declared that

> the policy of the government of the United States is to seek a solution which may bring about permanent peace and safety to China, preserve Chinese territorial and administrative entity, protect all rights guaranteed to friendly powers by treaty and international law, and safeguard for the world the principle of equal and impartial trade with all parts of the Chinese Empire.[9]

The American decision to become the champion of China was, second only to Monroe's commitment to defend the Latin-American republics, the most momentous event in our foreign relations.

How did Hay happen to make this commitment in the summer of 1900? The first clue to the answer is to be found in his action in the autumn of 1899 when he sent diplomatic notes to the six powers interested in

[9] Circular note to Austria-Hungary, France, Germany, Great Britain, Italy, Japan, and Russia. (William C. Johnstone, *The United States and Japan's New Order*. Oxford University Press, New York, 1941, p. 122.)

China [10] asking for the maintenance of what was called the Open Door for commercial interests in respect to equal tariffs, railroad rates, and port dues [11] in their Chinese spheres of interest. Although, after receiving their replies, Hay announced that the powers had come to a "final and definitive" agreement, and his achievement was hailed by his predecessor, William R. Day, as "a diplomatic triumph of the first importance," the replies had actually been in some instances conditional and evasive.

He was unable to do more at that time because of the crushing defeat of China by Japan in 1894–1895, which had wrecked the so-called Middle Kingdom. There was a vacuum opened up by the collapse of the Chinese government authority; the European powers and Japan were moving rapidly into it, and were establishing spheres of interest which meant the partition of China into a collection of colonies. [12] In a China which had been dismembered and reduced to colonial status, there could obviously be no Open Door for commerce.

[10] September 6 to November 17, 1899, to Great Britain, Russia, Germany, France, Japan, and Italy.

[11] But not — we must note — of investment and industry. (Samuel Flagg Bemis, *A Diplomatic History of the United States*. Henry Holt & Company, New York, p. 485.)

[12] On March 6, 1898, Germany took Kiaochow on the Shantung peninsula; on March 27, Russia took Port Arthur; on April 10, France took Kwangchow, and on June 9, Great Britain extended her holdings in Hong Kong and on July 1, took Weihaiwei. Admiral Dewey, we may note, fought the battle of Manila Bay on May 1 — while these events were happening.

But neither could there be peace, or law and order, or indeed satisfactory intercourse in a colonial China. The Chinese are too mature to tolerate it. The partition of China turned the Boxer Rebellion into an uprising against all foreigners, which became acute in May 1900. The legations of Great Britain, France, Germany, Russia, Japan, and the United States were besieged on June 20, and the siege was raised by an international relief expedition on August 14. The dates are significant. It was in July, during this siege, that Secretary Hay for the first time committed the United States to being the champion of Chinese unity and independence.

It seems clear that Hay's decision to oppose the dismemberment of China was based on a realization that, on the one hand, the Chinese would fight against partition and that, on the other, the United States would never achieve the Open Door if China was partitioned. That is how the American interest in China first became identified with the maintenance of Chinese independence.

We must fix clearly in our minds this fundamental fact — that what the Chinese did for themselves and what the United States has desired in China have in the past been reciprocal. We cannot understand why we are fighting in the Pacific, and therefore what we are fighting for, unless we remember how related, the one with the other, have been Chinese independence and American rights.

Why Americans should care so much about Asia as to fight a great war about it is a question that we shall have to examine thoroughly. But before we judge, we must first understand what happened.

3. *Rear-Guard Action over Forty Years*

From the time that John Hay proclaimed as American policy our opposition to the dismemberment of China until we were brought to war forty years later, the United States adhered to the principle but was unable to enforce it. Though Hay took the lead in 1899, he was relying upon British support. It is now known that the British had, in March 1898, made a formal proposal for joint Anglo-American action in China for the maintenance of free trade.[13] It may have been the influence of Alfred Hippisley, a British member of the Chinese customs service, that was decisive in Hay's mind.[14] Britain was by far the greatest of all the nations in the Far East,

[13] "On March 8, 1898, the British Government presented through Sir Julian Pauncefote its formal but secret proposal to Washington regarding the Open Door. White was at once told all about it. 'You will be interested to hear,' he wrote Hay, 'that Sir Julian Pauncefote's visit to the President of which so much was made in the papers, was to propose joint action in China for the maintenance of free trade to all the world, to which the President appears to have replied, with his usual prudence and reserve, most politely, but committing himself to nothing.' " (Allan Nevins, *Henry White: Thirty Years of American Diplomacy.* Harper & Brothers, New York, 1930, p. 163.)

[14] For the relations between Hay's American adviser, William W. Rockhill, and Alfred E. Hippisley, cf. A. Whitney Griswold, *The Far Eastern Policy of the United States.* Harcourt, Brace and Company, New York, pp. 62 *et seq.*

and it was not in her interest that China should be partitioned among the other European powers.

At the turn of the century the British imperial interest in China and the American interest in the Open Door, which as we shall see has very deep roots, happened to coincide. But it happened also that neither Great Britain nor the United States was then able to act as the champion of China. The United States was not a strong power. The Chinese government was helplessly weak. When in 1900 Germany decided to build a navy challenging British sea power in European waters, Great Britain could take no risks in the Far East, and she had at once to improve her relations with all the non-German powers. She came to terms with the United States over the Panama Canal.[15] She could not antagonize Russia, which was moving into Manchuria. She had to reinsure her naval position in the Far East by an alliance with Japan.

Thus Russia got new rights in Manchuria in 1901 and lost them to Japan in 1905. President Theodore Roosevelt, who understood the realities of power politics, gave way to Japan on Korea,[16] and had to accept the accom-

---

[15] Hay-Pauncefote Agreement.

[16] President Roosevelt expressed the view that it was useless to intervene in behalf of the Koreans for "*they could not strike one blow in their own defense.*" (Quoted by Alfred L. P. Dennis, *Adventures in American Diplomacy, 1896–1906.* E. P. Dutton & Company, New York, 1928, p. 416.)

By the Taft-Katsura Agreement of July 29, 1905, we had recognized that "the establishment by Japanese troops of a

plished fact in Manchuria. But what he conceded in fact, neither he nor his successors ever conceded in principle, and the integrity of China continued to be the grand objective of the United States in the Far East. When we had to, we chose to retreat rather than to fight. But we never agreed to change the American policy. And when we felt strong enough to insist on the policy, we did insist on it.

4. Why We Could Not Do More

For nearly twenty-five years, from the time the Manchu dynasty was overthrown by the rebellion of 1911–1912 until the end of 1936, China passed through an era of civil strife. During those years China was unable to achieve the unity and preserve the independence which the United States never ceased to insist upon.

It was during this period that Great Britain, France, and the United States were engaged in the First World War. Germany was ousted from the Far East and defeated in Europe, and Russia, defeated in Europe, was paralyzed by the bolshevik revolution. Only Japan, Great Britain, and the United States were then great powers in the Pacific and the Far East, and the United States was too isolationist and Britain too war-weary to

---

suzerainty over Korea to the extent of requiring that Korea enter into no foreign treaties without the consent of Japan was the logical result of the present war and would directly contribute to permanent peace in the East." (Dennis, *op. cit.*, pp. 428–429. From Tyler Dennett, *Roosevelt and the Russo-Japanese War*, pp. 112–114.)

maintain power capable of effective intervention in Asia. So Japan was free, though she was checked and restrained now and then, to extend her domination over China.

Nobody could oppose her. She therefore presented China with the ultimatum of May 8, 1915, demanding the acceptance of the Twenty-one Demands. China did accept, though Group V, which established an outright Japanese protectorate, was "postponed for later negotiations." While China was compelled to accept, the United States continued to object. President Wilson's Secretary of State, Bryan, and after him Secretary Lansing, said they could not "recognize" such agreements.

A few years later the United States emerged from war a great naval power, and at the Washington Conference of 1922 did induce Japan to quit Shantung, and to sign a Nine Power Treaty which again proclaimed the independence and integrity of China. By this treaty the powers for the first time bound themselves under international law to the American view of China.

Their commitments and ours as well were supposed to be covered by a collective agreement to consult. But there was no organization of power to maintain the treaty. On the contrary, at the same conference other treaties were signed which disarmed the United States to such an extent that we could not even fortify the Philippines and Guam, much less enforce our policy as far west as the China coast.

Because China was not united, she could do little for herself against Japan. In 1923 the Chinese revolutionary leader, Sun Yat-sen, turned to Soviet Russia for assistance.[17] He got it. The Kuomintang, his National People's Party, allied with the Chinese Communist Party and assisted by Russian advisers, organized the new Nationalist armies in Canton.[18] But neither the United States nor Great Britain had any taste for a Russified China, least of all a Russian communist China. In 1927 they intervened. They helped to split the Kuomintang from the communists, and even used their gunboats to shell certain cities held by the Chinese communists. The Russians were expelled. But China was divided. The Chinese communists set up a soviet in Kiangsi province; the Kuomintang set up its government in Nanking.

This divided China was beginning to unite when in 1931 Japan — in order to prevent the complete unification — amputated Manchuria from the rest of China. Though the United States took a strong diplomatic line, it was certain that the United States did not mean to fight. No one else was willing to fight, not even China, and Japan knew it.

What we might have done, what the League might then have done, if China had been able and willing to fight, no one can say. The fact is that China did not resist, and this is a sufficient and conclusive reason, far more significant than any other reason, why Japan was

[17] Soviet policy was then based on the design of world revolution. Cf. Chapter XI.

[18] George E. Taylor, *America in the New Pacific*. The Macmillan Company, New York, 1942, p. 120.

not stopped. For while it is often said that the League of Nations did not stop Japanese aggression, the deeper explanation, I believe, is that a nation which does not fight for its own unity and sovereignty cannot be endowed with these attributes of nationhood by others. The world can help only those who help themselves, and what we call collective security can only *reinsure* the security of nations and groups of nations.[19]

5. *The Turning Point*

Subsequent events, it seems to me, confirm this view. At the end of 1936, Chiang Kai-shek and the Kuomintang were compelled by the Manchurian troops to unite with the Chinese communists against Japan. It was this unification of the Chinese resistance that in July 1937 precipitated the present Japanese war against China. For the Japanese realized that if they were ever to conquer China they must conquer it before the Chinese were solidly united. A united China, such as we have always desired, would soon develop its resources, and would become invulnerable to Japan.

At the same time, this unification of the Chinese resistance led us to accept the risks of war on behalf of a principle which, though we had proclaimed it for forty years, we had never enforced. For when the Chinese were shedding their blood in behalf of that principle, we could not in honor and prudence stand aside.

[19] Cf. Part V, "On the Formation of a Universal Society."

Therefore, after a series of diplomatic protests, the United States began to take measures just "short of war." In July 1938 it laid a "moral embargo" on the export of aircraft to Japan. In July 1939, after the introduction of Senator Vandenberg's resolution,[20] Secretary Hull served notice that the commercial treaty of 1911 would expire at the end of six months. In the summer of 1940 the United States began to impose export restrictions which, though they were also designed to support the American armament program, brought a large part of our exports to Japan under control. In June 1941 an American political adviser was appointed by General Chiang Kai-shek; Americans were sent to reorganize traffic on the Burma Road; American aviators under General Chennault were allowed to resign from the United States armed forces and to volunteer with the Chinese Army. In August 1941, an American military mission under

[20] "Resolved, That it is the sense of the Senate that the Government of the United States should give Japan the six months' notice required by the treaty of 1911 for its abrogation, so that the Government of the United States may be free to deal with Japan in the formulation of a new treaty and in the protection of American interests as new necessities may require.

"Resolved further, That it is the sense of the Senate that the Government of the United States should ask that the Conference of Brussels of 1937, now in recess, should be reassembled to determine, pursuant to the express provisions of the Nine Power Treaty of Washington of 1922, whether Japan has been and is violating said treaty, and to recommend the appropriate course to be pursued by the signatories."

This resolution was never formally adopted, but an informal poll showed that the Senate Committee on Foreign Relations supported it. Senator Vandenberg has since said that his resolution was not meant to clear the way for an embargo against Japan. But at the time he did not disavow the action of Secretary Hull.

Brigadier General John Magruder was sent to China.[21]

On July 26, 1941, the United States froze Japanese assets in the United States for the purpose of bringing all transactions with Japan under the control of the government.[22]

This was a declaration of economic war. Along with the other economic and military measures taken at the same time by Australia, the Netherlands, and Great Britain, it was what the Japanese called it: an "anti-Japanese encirclement policy." [23] The chief of the Army Press Bureau at Japanese Imperial Headquarters declared that "Japan must break through the encirclement fronts by force." [24] We see, therefore, that the American decision to resist Japan was put into effect about four months before Pearl Harbor.

6. July 1941

We now have to understand why the United States waited so long. Why was July 1941 the date at which the United States accepted the challenge to all that it had contended for through forty years, and took measures which imposed the risk of war? There are naval officers of very high rank who hold that the issue should have been forced in December 1937, at the time when

[21] Taylor, *op. cit.*, p. 117.
[22] At the request of General Chiang Kai-shek Chinese assets were also frozen, but this was explained officially as being part of "this government's policy of assisting China."
[23] Goodrich, *op. cit.*, p. 508.
[24] *Ibid.*, p. 511.

the U. S. gunboat *Panay* and three American merchant vessels in the Yangtse River were bombed and machine-gunned by Japanese aircraft. They believed that Japan was not then prepared for war with the United States. They argued then, and still contend, that in a show of force over this incident we could have stopped the Japanese before they became irretrievably committed to the conquest of all of China; or, if we had fought then, we could have defeated them before Germany was ready for war in Europe. This may be the reason why the Japanese government apologized at once, and "later made full indemnification in accordance with the request of the United States." [25]

We need not try to decide now whether the government and the people were right to let the *Panay* incident be hushed up and settled with an apology and an indemnity. The fact is that when, on October 5, 1937, President Roosevelt had suggested a "quarantine" for aggressors — of which Japan was then a patent example — he had had an exceedingly unfavorable popular reaction. Shortly thereafter the German menace became so acute that not until the summer of 1941 did the world situation or the military position of the United States permit us to deal with Japan's ever-increasing violations of our rights and our principles.

The argument about the long appeasement of Japan, particularly with oil and scrap iron, must be judged in the light of the military position in the world as a whole.

[25] *Peace and War*, p. 53.

There was no large difference of opinion among responsible Americans that we wished to help China and eventually to stop Japan. The real difference of opinion was whether an effective embargo would paralyze Japan's capacity to wage war or whether it would precipitate war. The view which prevailed was that Japan would be ruined if a complete embargo was laid down. So she would fight because she would have to fight; therefore we must not lay down an embargo unless we were ready for war.

After the outbreak of the European war in 1939, we could not take the chance of a full-scale war in the Pacific until we were reasonably sure that Germany could not attack us through South America and in the Atlantic. The Japanese knew this. This was the grand strategy of the Axis. For Germany had been the unavowed ally and, since September 1940, the open ally of Japan. It was, therefore, not until July 1941 that the United States could lay an embargo which amounted to a declaration of economic war against Japan.

The Battle of Britain had not been won until May 10, 1941 — the date of the last big air raid on London.[26] Hitler turned east and committed his armies to the attack against Russia on June 22, 1941. Three months earlier, on

[26] The British Ministry of Information says that the Battle of Britain ended on October 31, 1940, when the Luftwaffe abandoned its attacks by daylight. But May 10, 1941, seems to me the more significant date, for then the Luftwaffe suspended large night raids as well.

March 11, Congress had enacted Lend-Lease, thus assuring the support of Britain, and eventually of Russia. Congress had adopted conscription in September 1940, but only by the summer of 1941 did the United States have any considerable army with as much as nine months' training. Congress had authorized a "two-ocean navy" in July 1940, but not until a year later was even a little of it built. Congress had appropriated large funds for industrial mobilization, but not until the summer of 1941 did American industry begin to produce munitions on any considerable scale. To have taken up the challenge of Japan's aggression in China any sooner than July 1941 would have meant accepting the risk of a great war in the Pacific before we had an army, an air force, and a war industry, or the foundations of a truly modern navy, and before we had the assurance that Great Britain and Russia could prevent Germany from attacking us in the Atlantic.

Even in July 1941 the risk was great. For it was by no means certain then that Russia could withstand the German attack. This risk, though very serious, had to be balanced against the risk of China's total defeat and the acceptance of Japanese domination by all the peoples of Asia. The American decision was fateful: it was determined by the fact that we could not challenge Japan *before* Britain had proved she could survive and before Germany was at war with Russia; yet we could not wait too long to take up the challenge of Japan lest China be conquered.

7. *The Final Showdown*

After the embargo of July 1941 the only question was when and where Japan would strike the blow that precipitated war. Since our strength was growing, the longer we could postpone hostilities, the better. Time was working in our favor and we had every reason for wanting to gain time. The Japanese were, of course, well aware of this. It now seems reasonably certain that early in November they began mounting their attacks against Pearl Harbor, the Philippines, Malaya, Hong Kong, and the Indies. They were ready for the war before the United States and Great Britain were ready.

It was under these circumstances that the final negotiations with the special Japanese envoy, Kurusu, took place, and the real issue was whether Japan could be appeased enough to postpone the attack for which she was ready and for which we were not ready. We have seen that the price fixed by Kurusu was that we should cease to help China and should assent to the Japanese conquest. This was the one thing we could not agree to. Yet if we could have evaded the issue even for a few months, or compromised it somehow, it would have been to our interest.

There is no evidence that the Japanese, who knew time was in our favor, would have been willing to let us evade and compromise. It was believed, perhaps for reasons which will not be fully known until the memoirs of the period are written, that if we had then sought again to appease Japan at the expense of China, the effect on Chinese resistance could quickly have become catastrophic. The Chinese were war-weary, weak, disorganized, and by no means solidly united. The alternative to resistance, if it seemed that no help would come from us, was for the Chinese to join the Japanese since they could not defeat them, and eventually to make a place for themselves in a new Far Eastern Empire. Wang Ching-wei, who is the Chinese puppet ruler set up by Japan at Nanking, was proposing this solution; he argued that the true course for China was to enter an Asiatic empire, to oust the Westerners, and to accept Japanese dominion under the banner of "Asia for the Asiatics."

The huge population and resources of China, organized and led by Japan, would have supported a combination of land and sea power in the Pacific which we could view only with profound alarm. In November 1941 we had to choose finally whether we would submit and let this Asiatic empire be established, or resist and go to war. If we appeased Japan further by not standing up to all we had said about China for forty years, we faced what was held to be the high probability that a Chinese government would be formed to come to terms with Japan, and that then, secured and reinforced in China, Japan would strike anyway and with much greater reserves of power.

Whether the Chinese ever put the matter before us that bluntly may some day be known. But the Chinese hardly needed to dot the *i*'s and cross the *t*'s in their official communications. All who were informed about the realities of the situation were aware that the risk we faced was that if we tried to temporize further, Chinese leaders would come forward to make terms with Japan. This was, I believe, the deciding reason why at the end of November, 1941, on the eve of Pearl Harbor — though we were not yet ready for war — the United States government felt it must reject the temporary compromise at the expense of China which Kurusu offered. Presumably this is what Kurusu had in mind when on November 26 he asked Secretary Hull whether our rejection of the proposed *modus vivendi* was "because the other powers would not agree." [27] The State Department's memorandum says: "but the Secretary replied simply that he had done his best in the way of exploration."

In the final showdown the United States judged that it had to accept the risk of immediate war with Japan rather than take the risk of a Chinese surrender followed by their collaboration in an Asiatic empire under Japanese hegemony.

[27] *Foreign Relations, op. cit.*, p. 766.

CHAPTER III

THE MYSTERY OF OUR CHINA POLICY

BEHIND all these events, which finally led to a war in which Americans are fighting all over the Pacific and in China, Burma, and India, there is a mystery which needs to be explained. How and why did the United States come to be so deeply concerned about the fate of an Oriental people from whom they are separated by the immense distances of the Pacific Ocean?

1. Was It the China Trade?

American interest in China originated in what President Fillmore called

the consideration . . . of the great trade which must at no distant day be carried on between the Western Coast of North America and Eastern Asia. . . . I need not say that the importance of these considerations has been greatly influenced by the sudden and vast development which the interests of the United States have attained in California and Oregon. . . .[1]

[1] Quoted in Nathaniel Peffer, *Basis for Peace in the Far East.* Harper & Brothers, New York, 1942, p. 39.

These words were addressed to Congress in 1849 in order to explain why the President had denied the French claims and had recognized the independence of Hawaii, then known as the Sandwich Islands.[2] The islands were regarded as a necessary commercial outpost for American trade. By 1840 Honolulu had already become a repair port for American whalers and the center of a three-cornered trade with China.[3]

The early exports to China were chiefly silver dollars and ginseng;[4] the imports were silk and tea. After 1790, or thereabouts, the Yankee merchants traded clothing, hardware, and other manufactures for sea-otter peltries in the Pacific Northwest, and then sold the peltries in Canton for silk, tea, enameled ware, and a yellow cotton cloth called nankeen. In 1818–1819 the value of the combined exports and imports was about $19,000,000: the

[2] Following the declaration by Secretary Webster in 1842 that the independence of Hawaii should be respected. (*Dictionary of American History*, "Hawaii." Charles Scribner's Sons, New York, 1942.

[3] Missionaries from Boston were sent out as early as 1820.

Originally, the trade with China itself was carried on both across the Pacific and across the Atlantic, around the Cape of Good Hope, across the Indian Ocean, and by way of the Dutch East Indies to Canton. Canton was the only Chinese port open to foreign trade until after the Treaty of Nanking in 1842. (*Ibid.*, "China Trade.")

[4] A plant which grew in the Hudson River Valley, and was believed by the Chinese to be a good medicine. A cargo of ginseng sent by Robert Morris in the ship *Empress of China* netted a profit of $30,000 in 1784. (*Ibid.*, "Ginseng.")

risks were great and the profits of this China trade were high.

This old China trade came to an end in the 1850's, and for about half a century,[5] until the 1890's, there was little American interest in that or any other foreign trade. This was, of course, the period of the Civil War, the Reconstruction, the settlement of the Western country, and the industrialization of America. But, as Peffer points out, when the transcontinental railroads had been built and the bonanzas had been staked out, the free land was gone and manufacturers were looking for markets. Then the American interest in "the great trade" with East Asia revived.

On July 7, 1898, during the war with Spain, Hawaii was annexed, and on December 10, 1898, the treaty in which Spain ceded the Philippine Islands was signed.[6] It is clear that the paramount consideration in taking the Philippines was the belief that Manila would be an entrepôt for the China trade. Strategic considerations of military power in the Pacific appear to have played no part in the mind of President McKinley and his advisers; this is evident from the fact that they were not sure whether they wanted *all* of the Philippine Islands. Not even Admiral Mahan, the great exponent of sea power, objected when Spain sold the Caroline Islands to Germany.

[5] Cf. Peffer, *op. cit.*, p. 45.
[6] Other outlying islands were ceded by another treaty, November 7, 1900.

Yet the China trade was never very large. At no time has it amounted to as much as 4 per cent of our whole foreign commerce.[7] Until 1860 the trade with Cuba was almost twice as valuable as the China trade. From 1861 to 1938 the China trade was about 3 per cent of our total trade; our trade with Japan was about 5 per cent of the whole; that with the British Empire, including Canada, was over 40 per cent.

Although our interest in China grew to be a vital interest, it was not because of the profits of the China trade.

2. *The American Meaning of the Open Door Policy*

Yet from the earliest days we have contended for an Open Door, so that American traders would have the same commercial rights as those of any other nation. Dennett shows that the policy of the Open Door is as old as our relations with Asia, that it was not limited to China, but was upheld also for Japan and Korea, and on the coast of Africa as early as 1832.[8]

The ardor with which Americans have espoused this principle is the heart of the mystery. The importance to the American people of the whole Oriental trade was, as we have seen, small. The merchants and the investors directly concerned in it could have done fully as well for themselves, probably much better, by entering into combinations with other nations for the colonial exploitation

---

[7] Cf. Bemis, *op. cit.*, pp. 307 and 759.

[8] Tyler Dennett, *Americans in Eastern Asia*. Barnes and Noble, Inc., New York, 1941, vii *et seq.*

of China. During the past generation, certainly, Japan would have been only too pleased to take the United States into a business partnership, provided we assented to her political domination of China. Had profits been the determining motive, Americans could have had them without the risks of war.

Yet, with deviations from the main line of our principles, which were soon corrected, Americans preached the Open Door incessantly to the other nations, and whenever the Chinese asserted their own independence, we gave them moral and material support. It is evident that the Open Door meant something more to Americans than a commercial policy, and that the missionary zeal with which we have propagated it touches chords of memory and of faith, and is somehow the expression of the American political religion.

The explanation is not far to seek. The American nation was born in a rebellion by the colonists against the mercantilist empire of Great Britain. The Open Door is simply a short name to describe American opposition to the trade monopolies and privileges of the mercantilist system. In the struggle for independence the American people acquired an indelible antipathy to monopolies and privileges established by imperial rule. Thus Americans react by long tradition, which is now well-nigh instinctive, against colonial imperialism. When they have themselves acquired colonies, as in the Philippines, they could not rest until they had promised the colonies independence; they were glad to provide the means by which the colonies could achieve independence; and the great majority were pleased when Congress, yielding to the pressure of the sugar lobby and the like, fixed a definite date for Philippine independence.

The American antipathy to imperialism is not a humanitarian sentiment acquired in some casual way. It is organic in the American character, and is transmitted on American soil to all whose minds are molded by the American tradition. It is a deep and pervasive habit of thought because it comes directly from the original conflict in which the colonists became Americans. That explains the missionary zeal with which Americans have championed what is apparently a merely commercial policy. English mercantilism, says Miller, "required the colonies to send many of their most important raw products to Britain and to purchase almost all their manufactured goods in the same market." [9] . . . Towards the end of the colonial period "the British government sought to tighten the screws of commercial monopoly . . . and even the staunchest defenders of colonial liberty in England, including William Pitt, insisted upon keeping the colonies in economic leading strings." The revolt against this system, and against the police measures used to enforce it, shaped the American conception of liberty and the rights of man.

Yet even after the outbreak of hostilities in 1775, the immediate object of the colonists was not independence;

[9] John C. Miller, *Origins of the American Revolution.* Atlantic–Little, Brown, Boston, 1943, p. 7.

it was the recapture and the propagation of English liberty. They declared their independence more than a year *after* they were at war and not until they were convinced that only through independence could they achieve liberty.[10]

Many of the patriots had a "veneration for the British Empire" which was "based upon the belief that it stood for liberty and the rights of man." Benjamin Franklin, who embodied the highest common sense of the patriot leaders, believed until the eve of independence that the best hope of human liberty lay in the extension of the English constitution. He advised Englishmen to recognize gracefully the potentiality of American growth, to make no laws which would hinder American trade and manufacture. He told them that their laws would be swept aside. He pleaded with them to think in terms of an Atlantic World, peopled by Englishmen, who, whether born in England or America, possessed equal rights and privileges.

But in 1775, writes Miller, "instead of founding the empire upon liberty and human rights," as enjoyed by Englishmen in England, "British imperialists thought almost exclusively in terms of revenue and enforcement of the Laws of Trade, and by their efforts to tax the colonies raised the question 'whether the rising empire of America shall be an empire of slaves or freemen.'" As a result, the colonists lost all their enthusiasm for extending the British Empire over the world. They

[10] *Ibid.*, p. 437.

turned to the idea of creating in this hemisphere a new world. "Here a new civilization was to be established while Europe sank into slavery. Only through independence, it was contended, could America attain its destiny and become . . . what Great Britain refused to be: 'the Glory of the World and the Terror of the Wicked Oppressors among the Nations' (*Boston Gazette*, August 24, 1772)." [11]

The success of the Revolution meant, of course, that the monopolies and privileges of the British mercantilist system were abolished on American soil. The merchants and manufacturers who carried on American business practised what it is now the fashion to call "free enterprise." When they sought for themselves, as indeed being human they often did, governmental favors, or when they formed monopolistic combinations, they quickly encountered the indigenous American radicalism which has always had as its watchword "Equal rights for all, special privileges to none." There never was established on American soil a ruling class which had recognized legal privileges. Consequently, though wealth has exercised much power, no hereditary governing class could be founded. The one notable exception was the great plantation owners of the South and their "peculiar institution" of chattel slavery.

Now without a hereditary governing class it has always been impossible for long to govern an empire: imperial rule over alien peoples abroad is vigorous and

[11] *Ibid.*, p. 437.

long-continuing only when there are great families which possess at home the traditions and prerogatives of governing others.

Having no ruling class which could administer an empire, the Americans have in the end always been anti-imperialists abroad: that is, they have disliked to see peoples ruled by alien powers. "Sometimes," said Jefferson, "it is said that man cannot be trusted with the government of himself. Can he, then, be trusted with the government of others? Or have we found angels in the forms of kings to govern him? Let History answer this question." [12] This is the spirit which has made Americans the missionaries of the Open Door. As Dennett says, "they desired to see the Asiatic states sustained and made strong to withstand by their own might the encroachments of European powers." The Open Door is, at bottom, a short name for the American way of life, projected abroad; the support of China by Americans, and their sympathy with all other colonial peoples seeking independence, reflect the fact that Americans, being incapable by the nature of their own society of sustained imperialism, are the opponents of imperialism wherever they encounter it.

For intuitively Americans have always felt, however little they measured the risks and were prepared for the costs, that they could not prosper and live securely in contact with states where governments worked on principles radically different from their own. They have

[12] First Inaugural, March 4, 1801.

believed profoundly that their own principles of liberty were founded upon the laws of nature and of nature's God, and that at last they would prevail everywhere. I believe that the history of our relations with Eastern Asia has proved that these convictions are the mainspring of the foreign relations of the United States.

The contrary view, that it is no concern of the Americans what happens in any other country, is not the normal American way of thinking. The Monroe Doctrine, which antedates our China policy by more than three quarters of a century, is founded on the open avowal that the principles of national freedom may not be attacked in this hemisphere by the great powers of the earth. Nothing could be further than this from the idea that what goes on outside our borders does not concern us. The argument that nothing abroad really matters vitally has frequently been advanced in controversies, but almost always as a reason for not taking some particular step on which men's judgments differed — as, for example, during Washington's administration over intervention on behalf of revolutionary France, in Lincoln's over support of the Polish insurrection, in Wilson's and Franklin Roosevelt's over intervention in Europe.

There have never been many isolationists who were so consistently noninterventionist that they did not at least vent their feelings by uttering ardent views about the internal affairs of other countries: about British rule in Ireland or India, Turkish rule in Armenia, Spanish rule in Cuba; about czarist and bolshevist rule in Russia, the Kaiser's and Hitler's in Germany. In fact, no other nation in modern times has ever preached so much about, or has passed so many judgments upon, the affairs of so many other peoples.

This persistent evangel of Americanism in the outer world must reflect something more than meddlesome self-righteousness. It does. It reflects the fact that no nation, and certainly not this nation, can endure in a politically alien and morally hostile environment; and the profound and abiding truth that a people which does not advance its faith has already begun to abandon it.

CHAPTER IV

THE WARS WITH GERMANY

IN THAT part of the world which surrounds the United States — in North and South America, in Eastern Asia, and in Western Europe — the United States has long made its presence felt, and what goes on within this region concerns us vitally. For the Monroe Doctrine, for the territorial integrity of China, for the defense of Western Europe, the United States has in the end been willing to go to war.

Beyond this oceanic region the United States has not had the same concern. India, the Middle East, Central and Eastern Europe, and the interior of Russia, have been outside the orbit of American vital interests. Our foreign relations have been with our more immediate neighbors within and across the two oceans.

Americans have, of course, long since realized that even within the oceanic region of the earth it would be quixotic, and almost certainly obnoxious, to go crusading in order to impose American institutions and the American ideas of liberty and equal rights. We have learned how far we are from having the right to set ourselves up as a model to our neighbors. And we have come to realize how long and troubled is the road to freedom and self-government — in Asia, in many parts of the Americas, and indeed everywhere. But we do react sharply and violently against acts of aggression which, if they were consummated and recognized, would foreclose the chance of our neighbors to develop in freedom. Thus the Monroe Doctrine is not a guarantee that all the people of the American republics will enjoy freedom; it is a policy which vetoes the attempt of any other power to prevent them from trying to be free. We have not undertaken to unite the Chinese and to make them free and self-governing. Only the Chinese can do that. What we have undertaken is to prevent Japan from conquering them. We have twice gone to war with Germany to prevent her from conquering Western Europe. Always our object has been not to impose our own dominion, but to prevent conquest.

1. The Second German Challenge

The calendar of events which have twice led up to war with Germany demonstrates that the instinct of national self-preservation is aroused in this country by successful aggression against countries on the opposite shores of the oceans which surround us.

Whatever some or many of our people may say, this is the danger to which the nation reacts. Men may call themselves isolationists or interventionists, nationalists or internationalists; they may be for neutrality laws or collective security, but their arguments subside when the nation sees itself facing a conquering power across its oceanic frontiers. Indeed when the arguments are examined closely, it becomes evident that they arise in the main from differing practical judgments as to whether the conquest of one of our neighbors will actually be achieved. If and when there is no longer any doubt, the American people react with remarkable unanimity.

The nazi regime came to power on January 30, 1933, and very soon showed its character by destroying German liberties, by glorifying war, and by menacing its weaker European neighbors. But although all this aroused protest, we must note that the rearmament of Germany, the remilitarization of the Rhineland in 1936, the conquest of Austria in 1938, the dismemberment of Czechoslovakia in 1938, its total occupation in 1939, and the invasion of Poland in 1939, did not cause the Administration to ask for, or Congress to take, any important measures to arm the United States. The nazi aggression appeared to be directed towards the east, away from the oceanic world.

While the nazis were generally execrated in the United States, only those who believed that Hitler would eventually turn west called for practical measures against him. And all they asked for at first was the repeal of the embargo on the sale of arms to Britain and France, and for giving the Western European nations the right to buy arms for cash and to carry them away at their own risk. No serious American armament program was proposed in this country even after the war in Europe had begun; as late as March, 1940, on the eve of the great German campaign of conquest in the west, the military appropriations asked for by the Administration and voted by Congress were somewhat above, but not much above, the peacetime level. "At the outbreak of the European war the President issued a limited emergency proclamation, in which he authorized an expansion of the active army from 210,000 to 227,000 men, and an increase of the National Guard to 235,000 men. . . . As late as March of 1940 War Department estimates for a small number of replacement airplanes were cut by the House of Representatives to 57 planes. An estimate of $12,000,-000 for the development of a defensive force in Alaska was refused."[1]

I am not discussing here the shortsightedness of our conduct, for my present concern is not to judge or to recriminate. It is to demonstrate objectively the thesis that this nation regards itself as vitally threatened only when aggression strikes into the oceanic region.

As compelling evidence that the thesis is true, we may note that as long as the land power of Germany was contained behind the barrier of British-French arms, and of Norwegian, Belgian, Dutch, Swiss, and Italian neutrality, German aggression was not treated as an actual and direct threat to the security of the United States. While this western barrier was still intact, the United States did not even prepare for war.

[1] *Biennial Report of the Chief of Staff of the U. S. Army,* July 1, 1939–June 30, 1941, pp. 2–3.

But when Germany breached the western barrier, there was an instant and virtually unanimous recognition that the country was threatened. The indisputable proof is that the isolationists no less than the interventionists started at once to arm the nation.

Germany invaded the Low Countries on May 10, 1940. The Netherlands Army capitulated on May 14, the French line was pierced at Sedan on May 14. On May 16 the President asked Congress for supplemental defense appropriations of 896 millions, and called for the production of 50,000 military planes — a program then generally regarded as unattainably large.[2]

The new defense program was called for because the Western European barrier had been breached. The unanimity with which the country recognized the danger of Hitler's assault on Western Europe is shown by the votes in Congress: the First Supplemental National Defense Appropriations Bill passed the House by 402 yeas, one nay, 28 not voting, and the Senate without a division.

The Belgian Army surrendered on May 28, and the British Army was evacuated from Dunkirk on June 4.

On June 10, Italy declared war. On June 14 the Germans occupied Paris. On June 22 Pétain's government surrendered at Compiègne. In July Congress passed without a dissenting voice in either house a bill to authorize the construction of a "two-ocean navy."[3]

[2] For text see *The Public Papers and Addresses of Franklin D. Roosevelt*. The Macmillan Company, New York, 1941, p. 202.
[3] Pub. no. 757.

Hitherto, the United States Navy had been designed for a one-ocean war in the Pacific against the Japanese Navy. A second navy in the Atlantic was not even authorized, much less built, until the German Army had reached the shores of the Atlantic Ocean and was believed to be ready and able to invade the British Isles and to capture the home bases of the British Navy.

Though there were some who continued to believe that Germany on the Atlantic seaboard was no serious threat to the Americas, the overwhelming votes of Congress contradicted them. When Germany reached the Atlantic seaboard, no responsible person dared to take the risk of not augmenting greatly our armed forces. The military power which Congress and the country had deemed sufficient while Britain and France held the Atlantic seaboard was at once judged to be wholly insufficient when the German Army reached it.

Now when a nation arms itself against another nation, then, no matter how fervently it hopes to stay out of war, it is declaring that it regards war with that nation as a practical possibility.

Therefore, when in 1940 Congress voted for a two-ocean navy, for a much enlarged army recruited by conscription, and for a great air force, Congress committed itself to the view that the German conquest of Western Europe was a threat to the United States. Lend-Lease and other measures to reinforce Great Britain and the whole resistance to Germany were the logical consequences of the earlier and primary decision to arm the United States. If the defeat of France called for greatly increased American armaments, then it would have been an absurdity not to aid Britain to prevent Britain's being defeated. And on the simple rule that the enemies of our enemies are our allies, it would have been an absurdity not to aid Russia.

I realize that this analytical interpretation of the causes of the second German war omits the moral issues between the nazis and their victims. I have not dwelt upon them because the record shows that in fact the evil character of the nazi regime was not the primary cause of the conflict between Germany and the United States. The nazi regime was as evil from January 1933 to May 1940 as it was afterwards. But it was in May 1940 that the United States began to arm in self-defense against Germany, and the occasion of its arming was when the German Army reached the Atlantic seaboard.

If the nazi regime had not been the evil thing it is, would the United States have reacted as it did react to the conquest of France? The answer to that question was given in the first German war.

2. The First German Challenge

The Germany of the Kaiser William II was not nearly so evil a thing as Hitler's Germany. But it had the same fundamental design of conquest — to be the master of Europe. This design caused it to violate the neutrality of Belgium, to invade France with the intent of crushing

her, and to besiege Britain with submarines in order
to ruin the British power. A German victory in the First
World War would have meant the establishment of an
empire from the Ukraine to the Iberian Peninsula, and
the dismemberment of the British Empire.

To this threat the United States reacted in 1917 as it
did in 1941. When, but only when, the Russian armies
had been defeated and Germany had a free hand for the
full conquest of the west — when, but only when, the
French Army was known to be in dire straits — when,
but only when, the submarine campaign appeared likely
to isolate and to destroy Britain — did the United States
refuse to compromise any further on the specific issue
of the violation of its traditional right at sea.

President Wilson ceased to write notes of protest and
he delivered an ultimatum which meant war when it appeared likely that without American intervention the
Germans would conquer Western Europe. The governing principle of American behavior has been the same in
both the German wars and in the Japanese war: when
there was no longer any doubt that a new empire,
founded on conquest, would become an accomplished
fact unless the United States prevented it, this country
passed from words to deeds, from diplomatic protest to
military measures. In the American view, as it has been
applied in two wars with Germany and one with Japan,
the evil which must be resisted has been the conquest of
our neighbors in the surrounding oceans.

3. *The Partisan of Freedom*

That is what we objected to even when the nation was young and weak. The Louisiana Purchase came about because Jefferson would not have Napoleonic France, a great conquering empire, at New Orleans. The Monroe Doctrine was laid down because Jefferson, Madison, Monroe, would not have imperial Europe, which Jefferson called "the domicile of despotism," in South America; they saw the chance and seized it, knowing that Great Britain would support them, to "emancipate a continent at one stroke." [4] John Hay made the Open Door and the integrity of China an American policy because we objected to the dismemberment and subjugation of China. That was the irreconcilable issue with Japan. The American objection to the conquest of Western Europe was the irreconcilable issue first with the Kaiser and then with Hitler.

Within the region of the world which fronts upon the Atlantic and Pacific Oceans, the United States is the enemy of all conquerors and the partisan of national freedom.

[4] Jefferson to Monroe, October 24, 1823. John Bassett Moore, *A Digest of International Law*. Government Printing Office, Washington, D. C., 1906. Vol. VI, pp. 394–395.

CHAPTER V

THE PERIL INTO WHICH WE DRIFTED

THIS WAR has supplied compelling and final proof that in their deep-seated opposition to the conquest of their neighbors in the surrounding oceans, the American people are inspired by a true conception of their own vital interest. Time and time again, in season and out, we had protested against aggression and conquest: in 1940–1942 we found out how right we had been when we made our protests, how mistaken we had been not to be ready and willing to back them up. The war has shown that a power capable of conquest in any large part of this region of the earth very soon jeopardizes the immediate safety of the United States. Japan had organized a power capable of occupying the Philippines, of gaining a foothold in the approaches to Alaska, and of threatening Hawaii and even the Pacific Coast; Germany had organized a power which was just barely prevented from establishing itself in South America and on the approaches to the Panama Canal.

The kind of war we have had to wage shows that our fundamental judgments were true, and that in failing to support them with a well-designed and well-prepared military and diplomatic policy we came to the verge of an irreparable national disaster. What we said was correct. What we did was tragically late and insufficient. We talked loudly and we did not carry a big stick. Our policy was insolvent because our commitments were unbalanced. This habit of ours weakened our position throughout the long armistice.[1] We were too late to prevent this terrible war. We were unprepared for it when it came, and we have had to wage the war under extremely disadvantageous conditions.

We shall have profited by the experience only if we are able to use wisely the victory we shall win. To use *this victory wisely we have to define our war aims in such a way that at the end of this war we shall have the efficient means to maintain our vital interests under a settled national policy.*

1. Words without Deeds

The United States has had to begin waging war after our enemies had already conquered, though they had not yet consolidated, many of the lands and peoples of their new empires. We have had to cross the oceans in order to storm the beaches on the outer edges of their new dominion. Our strategy has been dictated by our defaults: it consists in repairing our mistakes.

Though the instinct of national self-preservation in the

[1] Cf. my *U. S. Foreign Policy*, Atlantic–Little, Brown, Boston, 1943.

end compelled us to resist, our unawareness of our vital interest caused us to avoid, neglect, and refuse the measures which, if taken earlier, would have involved a smaller risk and much less cost of treasure and of life. We allowed our present enemies to pursue their ambitions and to become committed to their designs. Then when their own pride and prestige were engaged, we put them on notice that they would encounter our opposition. They did not believe us. Because our opposition was instinctive and verbal, and not a true policy in which the means are adequate to considered ends, we were long satisfied to proclaim our views without gathering our forces to make them good. In effect, therefore, we advised our enemies to prepare for a war which we ourselves did not prepare for.

Our warnings to Japan were delivered with ever-increasing emphasis from September 1931 to the spring of 1941. We began a mobilization in the summer of 1940 which could not be partially completed, as all expert authorities knew, in less than two years, and could not become formidable in less than three years. Thus our military preparations were not nearly completed at a time when our diplomatic protestations were exhausted and had patently failed.

As a result our task has been to expel Japan from territories which she had already, over our diplomatic protest, taken. We have to undo what we did not prevent. We are fighting to recover all that from 1931 to 1941 we had objected to Japan's taking.

If we did not recover it the Japanese force which has already conquered the Philippines and threatened Alaska, Hawaii, and our Pacific Coast, would remain intact. Exploiting the immense man power of Eastern Asia and the riches of the Indies, Japan would become a military empire potentially much greater than our own. We realize clearly now what we dimly apprehended: that the liberation of China and of the conquered peoples and places is indistinguishable and inseparable from the defense of the United States. If it were not, we should not have to liberate them in order to defeat Japan.

2. The Cost of Inaction

Fundamentally, the security of the United States demands that we prevent the establishment of a conquering empire in any part of the great oceanic basin of the Atlantic and the Pacific. Eventually it will threaten us. Eventually we must resist it. Sooner or later we shall be at war with it. This is the final reason for the Monroe Doctrine, for our championing the independence and territorial integrity of China, and for our intervention against the Kaiser's Germany and Hitler's.

Since a conquering empire upon the oceanic shores is our inevitable enemy, those nations which resist conquest are our natural allies. Their freedom from foreign domination is a vital interest of the United States. Their quislings are traitors not only to their own countries but to the great oceanic community to which we belong. We can never, therefore, be the friends of a regime like that of Wang Ching-wei, or of Pétain-Laval, and in the end we must become the partisans of the patriot forces.

This is how we have to act. In the end this is how we do act. But the time when we act, and the effectiveness with which we are prepared to act, are a matter of life and death. In the Pacific we waited to act until after the Chinese patriot forces had been cut off from us, and for all practical purposes isolated — until the islands of the Pacific, including the Philippines, which are the stepping-stones to the China coast, had been occupied or enveloped. This meant that, before the war began, we had lost command of the ocean west of Hawaii and that we were then compelled to fight bloody and bitter campaigns on jungle islands and atolls in order to reach China and join hands with the Chinese patriots.

In the European theater the situation has been radically different. But the difference demonstrates the same thesis. While our command of the sea was for a time seriously impaired by the submarines, it was never lost, and the great transoceanic base, which is England, was intact. To appreciate what this has meant, we have only to imagine our prospects in the Pacific if we had had an ally as powerful as Britain, within twenty miles of the Japanese Army and within bomber range of Tokyo, between ourselves and Japan.

We might, however, have been cut off from Britain as we were cut off from China, and we might have been as isolated in the Atlantic as we were in the Pacific.

After the fall of France in 1940 the Germans had a good prospect of subjugating the British Isles. Had they won the Battle of Britain, there would have been no power left capable of holding them back, even temporarily, at the approaches to the Western Hemisphere. They would have dominated, or have occupied without resistance, Iceland and Greenland and Eire, the Iberian Peninsula, and the Portuguese and Spanish islands as far west as the Azores; North and West Africa, including Dakar.

They would, then, have held in their hands the steppingstones across the Atlantic to North and South America. For the outer defensive positions in the hands of the United States, Canada, and the American republics would have been on this side of the Atlantic — on a long and scattered line from Newfoundland to Bermuda, Puerto Rico, Trinidad, and Natal.

The vulnerable region of the Western Hemisphere is South America. There is no military power of the first rank in South America. There is not as yet a well-settled and integrated habit of government. The unity of the hemisphere is far from having been perfected. Therefore, South America could not have been counted on to make an effective resistance of its own. Lacking the means, it was not at all clear that if left to make their own choice, the leading South American republics would have had the will to resist. The enemy powers were strongly entrenched within the governing classes of many of the South American republics.

The defense of South America depended, therefore, upon the United States. But it was clear that the defense of South America by North America would have been inordinately difficult if the victorious Germans, leaders of a new order composed of Franco's Spain, Vichy France, and Mussolini's Italy, were allowed to choose the time, the place, and the manner of their infiltration and aggression upon South America. The distance to South America, and particularly to the richest and most vulnerable region around the River Plate, is much greater and more hazardous from North America than from Europe through Africa and the Atlantic islands.

In 1940, in fact, the United States did not have the power to intercept an amphibious invasion of South America. What power we had — and it was insufficient — was committed in the Pacific against Japan. So the fall of Britain would have laid South America as wide-open to German invasion as the Philippines and the Netherlands Indies were open to the Japanese invasion.

Once established in Brazil and the Argentine the Germans would have held both shores of the South Atlantic. Then nothing could have prevented them from building up land and air power for an advance to the Panama Canal and against our communications in the Caribbean. After that even the defense of continental United States would have been extremely difficult. Fighting alone, after the fall of Britain, against the combined power of Germany and Japan, could we have hoped for anything better than to ask for a dangerous truce or to fight an exhausting and interminable defensive war?

3. When We Were So Nearly Isolated

These dire results did not happen. But that they could have happened is not open to doubt. Had we waited as long as we waited in the Far East, the United States and Canada in North America would have been isolated, not only from Europe and from Asia, but from South America as well. All the oceans would have been controlled by a coalition of our enemies. We should have stood alone, besieged, blockaded, on the defensive, incapable of taking the offensive, waiting until our enemies decided when and where they would strike at our inner defenses, and our own land.

This mortal peril was averted because in the most fateful months in our history Churchill's Britain fought off the Germans successfully in Europe and because the Americans who followed Roosevelt and Willkie prevailed. In the very nick of time the United States reinforced Great Britain. Even before we were able to send substantial reinforcements, we sent the tokens, guns for the defense of the island, destroyers for the support of the navy. With them we gave to the British nation hope that they would survive and in the end would triumph.

Thus there was held for us in the Atlantic what was lost to us, even before we began to fight, in the Pacific.

We held the command of the seas. The British Isles did not fall. Because they did not fall, the British, the Fighting French of General de Gaulle, the Belgians, the Dutch, the Norwegians, the Danes, the Greeks, the Yugoslavs, and the Poles resisted the German conquest. From the British Isles, and with American assistance, the power was mobilized to hold a ring of strong points around the Nazi Empire; what would we have given for the like around the Japanese Empire? We held Iceland. We kept Germany out of the Azores. We held Gibraltar, Malta, Egypt, and Suez. We held the North Atlantic passage to Russia. We held the South Atlantic passage to the Indian Ocean, the Red Sea, and the Persian Gulf. We held the airways from North America to South America, across French and British Africa to the Middle East, to Russia, to India, and to China.

All this we should have lost had the British Isles been allowed to follow metropolitan France and be defeated, had we stood by and let Churchill's government be overthrown, and a Mosley set up in Downing Street. If we had not intervened in the Battle of Britain, we should have lost practically all means of going to the assistance of Russia or of China. For the main assistance we have been able to send to Russia, or to China, has been carried over routes that Great Britain has held.[2]

When, therefore, it is said that in Europe we are fight-

[2] Though aid has gone to Russia by way of the North Pacific, there is no doubt that Japan would have closed it off if Russia had not been greatly reinforced elsewhere.

ing Britain's war, the answer is that if we had not helped Britain to fight her war, if we had let Britain become isolated as we did China, we should have had no possible way of fighting beyond our own shores. For the reinforcement of the defense of Britain was not only the defense of the North Atlantic and the South Atlantic approaches to this hemisphere; it was also indispensable to our being able to reinforce China and Russia.

Without Britain, without Russia, and without China, we should now face alone the joint power of the two most formidable conquering empires which have ever been established within striking distance of the United States. If Britain and Russia had been defeated in Europe, and had capitulated as France capitulated in 1940; and if China had capitulated in 1941 because we had continued to appease Japan, what would have been our prospects in the Pacific? With China, Russian Siberia, and British India at the mercy of Japan, and even through puppet governments allied with Japan, the Japanese rear in Asia would have been secure; an immense reservoir of man power and material would have been at her disposal. What would have been our prospects in the Atlantic? The whole of Europe and Russia and the Middle East and Africa would have been available for the Germans to mobilize and to exploit. In North America there are, all told, only 150 million people.

From the summer of 1940 to the summer of 1942 this country was in greater peril from more formidable enemies than it has ever been before. While we debated whether we wished to be isolated from our allies, we were in mortal danger of being isolated by our enemies. Not until we have measured that peril correctly, and have understood the causes of it, are we qualified and prepared to define our war aims. For our war aims are meaningless unless we can prevent this country from drifting into another such terrible predicament.

PART TWO

The Great Communities

CHAPTER VI

OUR CITADEL OF SECURITY

THE VULNERABLE side of the Western Hemisphere is in the Atlantic, which, as compared with the vast distances of the Pacific, is a small body of water.[1] We have had to command the Atlantic to reach our ally Great Britain; more than half the reinforcements we have sent to Russia have crossed the Atlantic; and for a long period between the fall of Burma until late in 1943, the bulk of the material we sent to China had to cross the Atlantic. This ocean is now an inland sea of the strategical system of security to which we belong.

This analysis has dwelt upon the peril in which the United States found itself when the nations of Western Europe were so nearly conquered by Germany. But it is equally important to stress the fact that all of Western Europe was very nearly conquered when the United States was neutral. The United States is now the inner citadel, within which there are the main arsenals and the strategic reserves of power for the defense of the

[1] "Among all oceans, the Pacific is outstanding. . . . The Pacific covers a third of the earth's surface. It is larger than the whole land surface. It comprises nearly half the entire water surface. The Pacific Ocean is over twice as large as either the Atlantic or the Indian Ocean." (Eliot G. Mears, *Pacific Ocean Handbook*, Stanford University, 1944, p. 1.)

whole region of the Atlantic. Twice within a quarter of a century we have seen that Western Europe has not been defended successfully without the support of the United States. These two wars teach us that Western Europe, North and South America, are for the purposes of security and defense one inseparable strategical system.

In this century the eastern frontier of this system has been at the western frontier of Germany, and, as we have seen, the breach of the barrier in the Low Countries and in France has been recognized, even by those Americans who were opposed to "intervention," as demanding an immediate mobilization of American military power. Whether the eastern frontier will continue to be where it has been for the past half century or more depends on the coming settlement with Germany. That is a question I should like to hold in suspense for the time being. But we shall come to it. It is enough to say here that the place of Germany in the international order cannot be determined until the order into which Germany is to be fitted has been settled.

For reasons which I hope to demonstrate clearly, an international order cannot be established in the modern world merely by a collective agreement among fifty or more individual national states: the order can be established only by the co-ordinated action of groups of national states. One of these groups I venture to call the Atlantic Community, and since we belong to it, it must naturally be our first concern. Even though it reaches far into the Pacific Ocean, I call it the Atlantic Community. For the power and authority of this community of states in both oceans, and of the civilization which prevails within them all the way to Australia and New Zealand, have their main source in the region of the Atlantic.

The settlements with Japan and with Germany cannot be made successfully by any one of the four great powers separately. Nor can the four together make a lasting settlement. Unless they are agreed not only with one another but with their neighboring states as well, all kinds of shifting combinations and permutations will occur, and the world will not settle down into an accepted order. The four-power alliance is not an international order; it is the nucleus around which order can be organized. To organize order we must begin somewhere, and the state of the world shows, I believe, that we must begin by defining, co-ordinating, fixing, and stabilizing the strategic defenses and the foreign relations of all states within the same strategical system.

The Atlantic Community is one such system. That Russia is the nucleus of another is clear, and China will form another. Eventually one or more constellations will probably form in the Hindu and in the Moslem worlds, but that is more distant. What we can recognize in detail even today is the grouping of the Atlantic Community on the one hand and of the Russian Orbit on the other. The settlement with Germany will be cemented by these two groups of states, with Japan by these two and China.

1. *One Military System*

We can be certain of the nations which are indispensable members of the Atlantic Community. They are Great Britain and France in Western Europe, the United States and Canada in North America. In time of peace these four nations may think they can go their separate ways. In war they need one another and are in mortal peril if they do not combine their forces. How many other nations adhere to this nucleus we shall see.

Because Britain was not able and the United States was not willing to support France when the French Army was still in being, British and American armies have to fight their way back over ground which, four years previously, was occupied not by German but by French troops. France has to be liberated in 1944 because France was not reinforced in 1939. We have to open a "second front" because we did not support the French front when it was still in being.

The interdependence of France, Britain, and North America is a demonstrated fact. Two tremendous wars are a demonstration which ought to be sufficient to convince anyone who will learn from experience rather than consult his prejudices. France could not stand without Britain. When France fell, the British Isles were in mortal peril. Britain could not stand without North America. If Britain had fallen, the Western Hemisphere would have been laid wide open. Had the Western Hemisphere been wide open, the United States would have had to defend itself in the Atlantic before it could have thought of resisting the Japanese conquest of China, the East Indies, the Philippines, and the Far Pacific.

The defense of each of these four Atlantic nations is inseparable from the combined defense of all of them. The acid test is not what men thought and said before the war. It is what happened. It is what they have had then to do, though tardily and therefore at greater risk and cost, when they were actually at war. In the two wars of our century these four nations on the shores of the Atlantic have had to fight under unified command; they have had to agree that each would provide the forces, the equipment, and the materials which, when combined, could be used in a common strategical plan.

The Atlantic Community is no figment of the imagination. It is a reality. We ignored and neglected it at our peril. Twice we have had to restore it at prodigious cost. In this war the community is operating as a single strategic and logistic system under the combined chiefs of staff. Their legal authority, and the material means at the disposal of the combined boards which are auxiliary to them, come from within the Atlantic Community. The combined command extends to the limits of the responsibilities and vital interests of this community.

Thus it does not extend to Russia or to China. They are allies in a world coalition. With us they are the founding members of a world order of peace. But they have conducted the war under their own strategic command, and they are separate, though related and co-ordinate, military systems. These are enduring realities that will shape the future, and no universalist formula can obliterate or alter them.

China and Russia are not members of the integral community of nations facing the Atlantic Ocean who must by the inexorable necessity of things *combine* for their security and their survival. We can come to good and solid terms with China and with Russia, but only by recognizing, not by ignoring, this reality. And certainly we shall never come to good and solid terms with them, nor could they come to such with us, if our own system, the Atlantic Community, disintegrates.

The burden of proof, then, is upon anyone who proposes to abandon the combined military system in the Atlantic World which has now been formed, and to which we and our allies owe our salvation and shall owe our victory. The opponent of maintaining the Atlantic system would have to show that an assault from without upon any member of this community would not be of vital consequence to all the other members. No one can show this. No one can show how Britain could live in security if France were not independent and her friend, or how Canada and the United States could live in peace if the Atlantic were an armed and disputed frontier and not an inland sea connecting them with dependable allies on the opposite shore.

2. *Rational Preparedness for War*

Since the region of the Atlantic is one defensive system, no nation within it *can* organize separately a rational and effective military establishment.

The first rule of reason, therefore, is that war *within* the Atlantic World is outlawed, and any idea of preparing for such a war should be excluded from all plans and calculations. This rule of reason has long been observed as between Canada and the United States. It ought to have been adopted by Britain and France, and by Britain and the United States. When in the twenties the British objected to a strong France, and when the British and American navies measured their relative strength as if they were potential enemies, we committed follies for which we have all paid an exorbitant price.[2]

[2] Cf. Memorandum by the Secretary of State on the Hoover-MacDonald conversations at Rapidan, October 5 to 7, 1929. "The President presented our proposition to divide the world into two hemispheres in the western one of which the British will not maintain naval or military stations which are a menace to us and in the eastern one of which we shall not maintain such bases which are a menace to them. They said that they were certain their existing bases in the western hemisphere were not fortified enough to constitute such a menace. It was agreed that only armament should be affected and not supplies or repairs. They were willing that the armament should extend only to the ability to stand off raids of privateers and to do ordinary police work against internal troubles. Finally it was decided that the best way was to have our General Board advise us as to the truth of the British statement that their bases are thus innocuous and

It would be equally foolish for the Netherlands and Belgium and Norway to build defenses against France and Britain, or for the Latin-American republics to build them against the United States. The security of the weaker members of the Atlantic Community lies in their becoming participating members of the defensive system to which they belong. Their contribution, in accord with their position and their means, to the common defense against attack from outside the community is the surest guaranty of their independence and their moral equality within the community.

For in isolation the strong can rarely, and the weak can never, long enjoy independence. Even Switzerland has been in mortal peril during this war, though by position and a long, unique tradition it is the most genuinely neutral state in the world. If Switzerland is an exception, there are no others — certainly not Eire or Sweden — to the rule that the security of a small state is in the combined security of its neighborhood. There is no doubt that Norway, Belgium, the Netherlands, and the American republics need to do what the most powerful states in their region of the earth need to do: to orient their military policy outward from the frontiers of the Atlantic Community, and not inwardly and within it.

The rule of reason that war is outlawed within the Atlantic Community is not a pious platitude. It is a most

---

then to have them agree not to increase them so that they would become a menace to us." (*Foreign Relations of the United States*, 1929. Vol. III, pp. 6–7.)

practical premise of policy. Had we known it and accepted it at the time of the Washington Conference in 1922, we should have been interested in seeing that Britain and France were strong enough, not in seeing how much we could weaken them. We should have made agreements to maintain our navies at an agreed level of power within the recognized theaters of possible war.

Upon this principle all the armaments of the Atlantic nations can in the future best be regulated. Instead of imposing a ceiling on the armaments of our allies and of ourselves, we shall need to establish a floor under us all. For each will have his responsibilities for the general security, and all of us will be concerned that all are capable of discharging them.

Since our forces, if they are ever used, will inevitably operate as a combined force, they cannot be effective in war unless they are designed with this end in view. So guaranties will need to be given and taken that each nation will maintain its agreed quota, that it will recruit and equip the kind of force which suits its capacity and fits into the general strategic plan of combined security. It will be necessary, then, to maintain combined staffs, intelligence services, and military planning boards.

It will also be necessary to make contractual arrangements for the mutual use of sea and air bases, and of many other military installations within the whole strategic system. No one nation within this region is strategically self-contained. The defense of South America, for example, cannot be conducted from continental United States; the operation involves French Africa, Brazil, the Portuguese and Spanish islands. The outer defenses of Britain and of France are in Norway, in the Netherlands, in Belgium, in Spain, Portugal, Italy, and North Africa. The whole region is so interlocked by the shape of the land and the sea within it that in time of war it is bound to be one single theater of combined operations. A rational military policy will, therefore, lead all the member states to standardize their equipment so that all their bases and installations are fitted for the conduct of combined operations.

If these principles are acknowledged, the military chieftains, the civil governments, and the legislatures will have a basis for calculating the proper size and character of their sea, land, and air forces. How else could our Navy Department, for example, tell the President and Congress why they are asking for a particular navy bill, rather than for one twice as big or half as big? Nothing can be calculated about the United States Navy unless we know where the British Navy stands. Nothing can be calculated about the size of our army unless we know what armed strength we can count on elsewhere.

A rational military policy for the United States can be founded only upon a solid political understanding that war within the Atlantic region is unthinkable and that war beyond it, and in defense of it, is certain to be a combined operation.

CHAPTER VII

THE ATLANTIC COMMUNITY

THE ATLANTIC nations should not have divergent foreign policies, since all are involved if any one of them is at war with a great power. A house divided against itself cannot stand. For this reason they need frequent consultations and must be in continual agreement on any measure which might involve them in war.

Complete uniformity in all their foreign relations is not necessary or desirable: France, for example, will have European connections that Canada, the United States, and Brazil do not have. But certainly it ought to be the rule that no Atlantic state shall make a new major commitment or shall renounce an old one without consulting the others.

1. Organic Consultation

A settled understanding, or compact of this kind, is in the vital interest of all the members of the Atlantic Community. It is very much our own concern, now that we find ourselves so close to the geographical center rather than on the periphery, as we once were, of the Western World. To this epoch-making change it is not only the United States that must readjust its whole conception of foreign policy: the other great powers of the Atlantic World, namely Great Britain and France, must also readjust their conceptions.

I am sure that no reader of this book[1] will think I share the view that in two great wars the United States has been pulling only the British and French chestnuts out of the fire. There is, nevertheless, pregnant truth in the persistent American feeling that twice we have had to help finish a European war of which the beginning was remote and obscure. The transatlantic nations can reply that after 1919 we, too, had our chance to prevent the beginning of a great war, but that we refused to take it. Many Americans will retort that they were invited by President Wilson to underwrite the consequences of a European diplomacy in which they did not in fact have an influence commensurate with the responsibilities they were asked to assume. . . . Our present concern is with the future, and we can agree, I think, on this: though we intended isolation, we were involved in world wars; therefore, in the future we shall need to exercise the rights of full consultation in all decisions that can lead to war. It follows that as the United States alters its isolationism, Great Britain and France will need to modify their habits of independent initiative and decision in great matters of foreign policy.

This view corresponds, I believe, not only to sentiment

[1] Cf. Chapter V.

and interest in the United States but also in Canada, Australia, New Zealand, and South Africa.[2] British statesmen are aware of it, as we know from an address by Lord Halifax [3] to a Canadian audience: —

> I speak frankly as I know you would have me speak. On September 3, 1939, the Dominions were faced with a dilemma of which the whole world was aware. Either they must confirm a policy which they had had only partial share in framing, or they must stand aside and see the unity of the Commonwealth broken, perhaps fatally and forever. It did not take them long to choose, and with one exception they chose war. But the dilemma was there, and having occurred twice in twenty-five years, it may occur again. That is the point at which equality of function lags behind equality of status. The Dominions are free — absolutely free — to choose their path; but every time there is a crisis in international affairs, they are faced with the same inexorable dilemma, from which there is no escape.

The United States has twice been faced with an inexorable dilemma of a similar kind — to reinforce Great Britain and France in a war which originated in Europe or to stand aside and see the historic defenses of the

---

[2] Cf. Robert MacGregor Dawson, *The Development of Dominion Status — 1900–1936.* Oxford University Press, London, 1937.

[3] Delivered at Toronto on January 24, 1944.

Western Hemisphere broken, perhaps fatally and forever. Moreover, the Latin-American republics have also
been faced with this dilemma, and the event has shown
how great a strain it places upon the solidarity of the
Western Hemisphere. It must also be said, and faithfully
taken to heart by Americans, that ever since 1922 when
the United States insisted upon the rupture of the Anglo-
Japanese alliance, Great Britain has been confronted
with another such inexorable dilemma in the Far East.

Though it is a delicate matter for an American to
discuss, it is apparent that the dilemma defined by Lord
Halifax cannot be resolved within the British Commonwealth alone. The United States, the other American
republics, France, the Low Countries, Norway, and
others as well, cannot be left out in framing the policies
which Great Britain and the Dominions adopt. It is not
likely, moreover, that the Dominions will ever again
feel that they can afford to follow a British Commonwealth policy, of which the issue might be war, without
the full agreement of the United States.

There is no alternative, so it seems to me, to the conclusion that the nations of the Atlantic Community will
have to stipulate with one another that they will pursue
a common foreign policy in their relations with the non-
Atlantic World. Such a common policy will require
what Mr. George Catlin has called "organic consultation": that is to say, something more elastic than a formal
treaty of alliance, and something much less than political

federation — a network of agreements and understandings that, as a matter of right, there will be a habitual exchange of information and views in the ordinary routine of the foreign offices, the war offices, and the departments and agencies which regulate international commerce.

2. *The Atlantic Charter: Its Domicile*

Our relations with the British nations, with France, with Western Europe, and with the other American republics, have become different in kind from our relations with the other great states beyond. Within the Atlantic Community the word "foreign" has to be radically qualified when we speak of foreign policy. For a truly foreign policy is one in which if diplomacy fails there may be a resort to force. But in their dealings with one another the Atlantic States can never resort to force.

The Atlantic nations remain separate sovereign states but they form a living community.

In respect to one another the principal Atlantic powers have long had settled frontiers. There are territorial disputes in South America, in Northern Ireland, and in North Africa. They trouble the peace. But they are not likely to engender great international wars. Among the leading military powers of the community there are no disputed territories about which they could conceive of going to war. Now in spite of all that has been written about trade rivalry and ideology as the cause of war, disputed land, especially if it is national territory, is much the most dangerous cause of war. In no other part of the world is there so settled a condition as within the Atlantic Community.

The Atlantic Community is an oceanic system: indeed, some might prefer to call it the Oceanic Community. The chief military powers within it are separated by water. In respect to one another they are islands. The North Sea lies between Britain and Scandinavia, the Channel separates Britain from France and the Low Countries. The oceans separate North America from Western Europe, from Africa, from South America, and from Australasia. This means that the community cannot be held together by military compulsion. It cannot be one military empire ruled from one capital.[4] It can be only a concert of free nations held together by a realization of their common interests and acting together by consent. This has been their individual weakness in dealing with Germany and Japan. The Atlantic nations have been free to go their separate ways until each in turn was threatened with destruction. But this freedom is their moral passport among the peoples of the earth, the guaranty that they will not unite for aggression and domination. They can unite only in self-defense.

[4] Cf. Ross J. S. Hoffman, *The Great Republic*, Sheed and Ward, New York, 1942, especially Chapter I on the deeply settled objection of Western man through the centuries to a world state.

The United Kingdom and France must stand together. But neither can compel the other to stand with it. Neither can occupy and dominate the other. Yet each must defend the other. Unless, however, each has the authentic will, authentically given because it is voluntarily given, their alliance will be perfunctory and undependable. So it is between the United States and the British nations. They must collaborate and they cannot be dragooned. So too with South America. The United States could not, even if it were so stupid as to wish it, occupy Brazil and the Argentine in order to compel them to act with the United States. Though the combined defense of North and South America is imperative, it can be achieved only by agreement. There is no way to compel agreement. It can be had only by the inducement of reciprocal advantage and the growth of a common loyalty.

Thus it is that in the Atlantic World the facts of international life conform with the spirit of the Atlantic Charter. Elsewhere non-aggression and non-interference may still represent an aspiration: a great number of new small states, none as yet well established and most of them with disputed frontiers, are appearing. The spirit of the Charter is a novelty in Eastern Europe, in Africa, the Middle East, and in Southern and Southeastern Asia. Here it will not always be easy to carry out the letter or the whole spirit of the Atlantic Charter. But in the Atlantic World the ideas of the Charter are familiar. Even though they are not completely realized, they do reflect what has now come to be in the main our real intent and the actual performance. So when the President and the Prime Minister gave name to the Charter which they proclaimed from the deck of a battleship off Newfoundland, they were, whether or not this was their intention, also describing its local habitation.

3. *The Good Neighbor Principle*

The Atlantic or oceanic region is that part of the world where the rights of small states — small as measured by power — are most secure. As a matter of fact, most of the well-established small states actually are in that region. In addition to the United States, the United Kingdom, and France, which are great military powers, the Atlantic Community includes the following states: Argentina (in spite of her dissent), Australia, Belgium, Bolivia, Brazil, Canada, Chile, Colombia, Costa Rica, Cuba, Denmark, Dominican Republic, Ecuador, Eire, Guatemala, Haiti, Honduras, Iceland, Liberia, Luxembourg, Mexico, the Netherlands, New Zealand, Nicaragua, Norway, Panama, Paraguay, Peru, Commonwealth of the Philippines, Portugal, Salvador, Union of South Africa, Spain, Uruguay, Venezuela.

We should also include Sweden (now a neutral), Italy (an ex-enemy), Greece (a recognized maritime state), and Switzerland (traditionally neutral), all of them vitally bound up with the Atlantic Community.

There are of course other small, yet important, states not within the Atlantic system of security. There are, for example, Czechoslovakia, Poland, Finland, Romania, Bulgaria, Yugoslavia, Hungary, and Austria. The vital strategic connections of these states are not with the Atlantic sea powers but with the land power of Russia.

In considering the future, we must recognize that the independence of the small states of North and South America has long rested on a quite different foundation from that which in the past preserved small states in Europe. In the New World there has been developed a relation between the great powers and the small nations which is happily and accurately named the Good Neighbor Policy. In Europe until the outbreak of this war, on the other hand, small nations staked their independence upon the maintenance of a delicately poised balance of power among the great states.

The foreign policy of Poland or Finland, for example, was not one of neutrality as Americans understand it. They hoped to survive by leaning on Germany against Russia and upon Russia against Germany. Disliking and fearing both their great neighbors, they sought to stand between them, aligning themselves definitely and finally with neither. They might have succeeded if, as was the case in the nineteenth century, a very great power outside of Europe, namely Great Britain, had been able to maintain the balance of power among the strong states of the Continent. But once Great Britain ceased to be strong enough to do this, the small nations of Europe were doomed to disaster if they continued to rely upon the balance of power. Their only hope of security lay in ceasing to play one power off against another and in aligning themselves definitely and conclusively with a neighboring great power.

Theoretically that power might have been Germany. But it could not be Germany because the indubitable object of the rulers of Germany was a European despotism — or as Hitler called it a New Order — in which the Germans were the master race and the small nations were German colonies. Therefore, the only course for the small nations of Western Europe would have been to align themselves with Great Britain and France, and for the small nations of Eastern Europe to align themselves with Russia. The proof that this was their right course is that only as the allies of Great Britain and of Russia in this war can they be liberated and have their independence restored.

In regard to Belgium, the Netherlands, Luxembourg, Norway, and Denmark, the demonstration is so conclusive that there is no present intention on their part to return to "neutrality" and to depend upon a balance of power. Their intention, fixed by the lesson of the war, is to pursue instead the Good Neighbor Policy with Great Britain and France — that is if Britain and France are willing to adopt it themselves.

In Eastern Europe the psychological difficulties of

such an alteration of policy are obviously much greater. But nothing is more certain in human affairs than that the small states of Eastern Europe cannot recover their independence and maintain it after this war by the wholly obsolete policy of trying to rely upon the balance of power. The Czechs have recognized this in their treaty with the Soviet Union. The Bulgars, by refusing to declare war against Russia, have shown that they are certain in the end to recognize it. Inordinately difficult though it now seems that the Finns and the Poles should also recognize it, the fact is that their independence cannot rest upon the military support of Britain and the United States. Their independence can rest only on a Good Neighbor policy in which they, for the sake of independence, and Russia, for the sake of her own security and the peace of the world, come to terms.

The Good Neighbor principle has now been applied long enough in the Western Hemisphere to enable us to see what concretely it means. It is, as the name indicates, a policy of non-aggression, co-operation, and good will. But it is not, as this might suggest, a sentimental and verbal policy. However little the realities which underly it are avowed, they exist and are controlling.

The Good Neighbor relationship is one in which small states and a great one in the same area of strategic security become allies in peace and in war. The great state provides protection which — the technology of modern war being what it is — no small state can provide for itself. The small state reciprocates: it provides strategic facilities needed for the common defense, and it uses its own sovereign powers to protect its great neighbor against infiltration, intrigue, and espionage. Insofar as the small state makes this critical contribution to the security of the neighborhood, its independence is of vital interest to its great neighbor. The stronger the small state becomes, the more vigorous its national life, the better neighbor it is. For a small state which jealously guards its independence against aggression from an enemy of the neighborhood is incomparably more useful than it would be if it were occupied and ruled by its great neighbor.

So when we say that we are the champions of the rights of small nations, we must particularize. We must add that they can now assure their rights only by a general acceptance of the duties of the Good Neighbor Policy. We must not, as many do, identify the rights of small nations with their right to have an "independent" foreign policy, that is to say one which manipulates the balance of power among great states. A policy of that kind may have been feasible in the confines of the little Europe of the eighteenth and nineteenth centuries. Yet we must remember that even then it ended in the partition of Poland. In this century small states are much too small in relation to the big ones to pursue any policy but that of the Good Neighbor.

This policy has been discovered and has been proved

— though it is far from perfected — in the New World, and Americans may advance it as a constructive contribution to the peace and liberties of mankind. We have been able to make this contribution because in the Western Hemisphere for more than a century there has been no such thing as a balance of power. That might, according to European experience, have meant the creation of an American empire. It has, instead, led to a radical innovation in human affairs, and to the only true substitute for empire, which we call the Good Neighbor Policy.

4. The International Exchange Economy

The Atlantic Community contains about 522 million people organized in about 42 sovereign states. The Soviet Union has 193 million in one sovereign state.[5] Thus we see how diffused is political authority within the Atlantic Community. As compared with the Soviet Union alone, the Atlantic Community is a very loose constellation. It consists of a large number of independent states. Because they are so many independent countries, none of the Atlantic nations, excepting only in some measure the United States, is even remotely self-sufficient. The consequence of so much political independence is a very high degree of economic *dependence* upon foreign trade.

[5] Population as of 1940. From *Political Handbook of the World, 1944*. Edited by William H. Mallory, Harper & Bros., New York, 1944.

The Atlantic region is the historic center of the international exchange economy. The bulk of the shipping of the world, the international commodity and money markets, and the colonial development of the world, have been managed by the Atlantic nations. Their dependence upon international commerce has stamped a special character upon their internal economies; this condition has promoted private trading and, therefore, private enterprise.

It may well be that after this war government regulation will be much more extensive. That is a question which lies outside the scope of this inquiry. Here we are concerned with American security and world peace, not with the social reconstruction which will be based upon security and peace. But it is relevant to our inquiry to note that even if the Western nations should abandon laissez-faire and manage their economies, the fact that there are so many of them would mean that each must manage its affairs in such a way as to maintain a high degree of initiative, individuality, and flexibility in its economic life. A fully regimented and planned economy is feasible only where one central authority is sovereign over an area which is for all practical purposes economically self-contained.

For all these reasons, the Atlantic region will, despite all changes in social organization, retain the essential political character which fits its way of life. With minor deviations the nations will adhere to their historic tradition: that the state exists for man, and not man for the state; that the state is under the law, not above it; and that the individual person has inalienable rights. No social regulation which violates these principles [6] will long be endured in the Atlantic World.

5. The Shape of Things to Come

The national differences within the Atlantic region are variations within the same cultural tradition. For the Atlantic Community is the extension of Western or Latin Christendom from the Western Mediterranean into the whole basin of the Atlantic Ocean. Its frontiers, which are a fluctuating and disputed borderland in Germany and Central Europe, still follow roughly the frontiers of the western part of the Roman Empire. Beyond the Atlantic Community lies a world which is still the heir of Byzantium. Beyond them both lie the Moslem, the Hindu, and the Chinese communities.

The problem of *world order* is, I believe, insoluble if we seek to constitute the order out of the sixty or more individual nations. It is soluble, I am contending, if the world order is composed of the great regional constellations of states which are the homelands, not of one na-

[6] For a fuller discussion of this theme, and particularly of how freedom, as men know it in the Western World, may be reconciled with the modern social order, cf. my book *The Good Society*, Atlantic–Little, Brown, Boston, 1943 edition.

tion alone but of the historic civilized communities. This is the shape of things to come. If we see this truth clearly enough, and are faithful to the promise which it contains, we shall create the security which is our national war aim, and the lasting peace which is the war aim of all civilized men.

CHAPTER VIII

BEYOND THE ATLANTIC COMMUNITY

OTHER REGIONAL COMBINATIONS are forming in the world, the most important being that of which the Soviet Union is the nucleus. The relations of the Atlantic Community with this system, which I shall call the Russian Orbit, will decide the outcome of the war both in Europe and in Asia, and the settlement for as much of the future as we can now foresee. The boundaries of the Russian Orbit are not clearly defined. But it certainly extends from Prague to Vladivostok, from Eastern Europe to the shores of Eastern Asia, and its heart is the Soviet Union.

1. The Russian Orbit

During this century Russia has fought two wars against Germany. These wars have convinced the Russians, and that is what counts in this matter, that the Western nations are unable to enforce peace east of the Rhine and to prevent a German invasion of Eastern Europe and of Russia. Therefore, the Russians are bound to consider the region eastward from Germany as a separate strategic system of security.

In 1914–1917 all of Central and Eastern Europe and the Balkans was overrun by Germany; Russia was defeated, invaded, and dismembered. Again in 1938, beginning with Austria and Czechoslovakia, Germany proved that the Western powers cannot protect this Eastern region. In 1941, for the second time in twenty-five years, Russia was invaded by Germany. Now no matter how high we rate the help that Britain and America have given Russia, the plain fact is that the expulsion of the German armies from Russian soil, and from Polish, Czechoslovak, Romanian, Finnish, and Bulgarian soil as well, depends preponderantly upon the Red Army and the exertions of the Russian people. It is, therefore, clear that Russia exists in and depends upon a region of strategic security separate from the Atlantic powers.

This does not mean that the Atlantic and the Russian regions are not interdependent. They are. It is evident that Russia alone could not have defeated Germany, and certainly not Japan as well. It is equally evident that if the Western nations had not been allied with Russia, they could not hope for a decision against both Germany and Japan. Upon these conditions rests the Western alliance with the Soviet Union. We all have the same enemies and without mutual aid none of us could defeat these enemies.

Our primary war aims are, therefore, the same. The conclusive defeat of Germany and Japan will make Russia invulnerable for as long a time as can be foreseen. The primary Russian war aim must be, in its simplest terms, not to lose the security which victory will have given her. This also is our first war aim. The conclusive defeat of Japan will make the United States and the whole Atlantic Community invulnerably secure in the Pacific; the conclusive defeat of Germany will make Western Europe and the Americas secure.

Quite evidently, the crucial question of how long and how confident can be the peace after this war will be determined by the maintenance of the substance of the alliance between the Russian Orbit and the Atlantic Community. Whether there is to be a third World War in the twentieth century depends upon whether the Russians come to rest within their orbit, the Atlantic States in theirs, and whether they then concert their policies towards Germany and Japan. We shall, therefore, return to the crucial question of our relations with the Soviet Union when we have discussed the settlements with Germany and Japan.[1]

I do not say that such a concert of power with the Russian Orbit is a world order of peace. But I do contend that such a concert must be achieved in order to found a world order. The concert, as we shall see, is absolutely indispensable to any lasting settlement with Germany and with Japan.

It is also necessary if there is to be any prospect of order and good relations with the emergent peoples of Asia and Africa.

[1] See Chapter XI.

2. *The Chinese Orbit*

China has two great neighbors. They are Japan and Russia. When we put away the maps of the age of sailing vessels and use a globe for our geography, we realize that to the heart of China the direct routes from the United States by air are over Russian territory, and that even by sea they pass through Russian and Japanese waters. Russia, and also Japan, are between America and China.

The course of this war has indicated how this bears upon China's position in the world. Japan was able to cut China's sea connection with the United States. Yet with little help from us the deep interior of China has long resisted Japanese conquest. If Owen Lattimore,[2] who is a tried and true friend of China, is right in thinking that the center of the China of the future will be not along the coast and the Yangtze River but in the deep western hinterland, that the industrialization of China "will be firmly built in the heart of the country," and that "from there it will expand back to the coast," then when China is freed of the Japanese menace, she will also be strategically independent of us.

When Japan has been defeated, China will necessarily look for her primary peace and security not across the Pacific to us, but backwards, so to speak, across the

[2] Owen Lattimore, *America and Asia*. Claremont Colleges, Claremont, California, 1943, pp. 36–40.

Eurasian land mass. China and Soviet Russia have an immense land frontier which runs for four thousand miles from the Pacific to the Pamirs in the very heart of Asia. Surely, Lattimore is right when he says that "the things that will happen along that land frontier, far beyond the reach of any American gunboat or battleship, or airplane carrier or air base . . . are of greater significance than anything that will happen in the Pacific Ocean."

Another regional system will form around China. That it will in time encompass not only the Chinese dependencies in the north but also the whole or the greater part of the mainland of Southeast Asia is probable. We cannot know how soon this will take place because we cannot know how soon China, freed of the menace of Japan and of the tutelage of the Western powers, will achieve her internal political unity and her industrial development. When she does achieve them, China will be a great power capable of organizing her own regional security among the smaller states of Indo-China, Burma, Thailand, and Malaya. China and the Soviet Union will have to come to terms along their great Asiatic frontier. The rise of China will also precipitate great questions for the British Commonwealth and Empire, and indeed also for the other Atlantic powers, including the United States. But these questions are not yet clearly posed, and though they can be foreseen dimly, they cannot yet be answered and settled.

3. *Emergent Asia*

It is equally evident that the future will bring momentous developments among the peoples of India and in the Moslem societies. We cannot see that future at all clearly. We might wish we could. But in truth we cannot in our own time settle everything for all time. All we can hope to do is to stabilize and organize as much of the world as is ready for it, and thereby make it easier for our children and our grandchildren to deal with their problems.

We must take it as decided that the tutelage of the Western empires in Asia is coming to its predestined end. We cannot doubt that the thousand million people of China, India, and of Islam will achieve an importance and a power they have not hitherto had in the modern world. But as the Western empires recede and before the newly independent states are well established, the peoples of Asia will almost certainly pass through a long interregnum. It will be a time of troubles. Only by a miracle can effective civil authority be established throughout Eastern and Southern Asia without prolonged and complicated civil and international strife.

The history of the Western World as a whole, and of each nation which has formed within it, teaches us what to expect. Possibly, but not probably, the peoples of Asia may learn so much from our long and hard history that their own will be easier. The Western nations have had to win, earn, and pay for independence, unity, self-government, and position in the world, by labor and hard experience, and with blood.

But of one thing we may be certain. It is that since the tutelage of the Western powers is ending, their influence even in guiding, much less in controlling, the evolution of Asia will become increasingly remote and indirect. Yet they must take what measures they can to prevent the emergence of Asia from disrupting the peace of the world. It will disrupt the peace of the world if the Soviet Union and the Atlantic nations become rivals and potential enemies in respect to China, India, and the Middle East. The emergence of Asia can also disrupt the peace of the world if the members of the Atlantic Community act separately. What France, or Great Britain, or the Netherlands, or Australia, does in respect to China, the Middle East, India, Burma, Malaya, and the East Indies can lead to consequences among the great masses of Asia that none of them, acting individually, might finally be able to deal with. Therefore, they cannot afford to adopt policies which will not surely command the support of the nations whose interests may also be involved. This means that colonial policy can no longer be the sole prerogative of the imperial state, and will have to be set by consultation and agreement.

PART THREE

The Settlement with the Enemy

CHAPTER IX

SETTLEMENT WITH JAPAN

IF A READER asks why a book on war aims has had so much to say about the Allied world, and nothing as yet about the settlement with our present enemies, my answer is that nothing can in fact be decided about Germany and Japan until we have made up our minds about what we can and should do with the alliance of the United Nations in the post-war period.

I am assuming that no responsible person wishes to dissolve it. Yet it is evident that when the fighting comes to an end the improvised war alliance will have to be transformed if it is to be stabilized. So I have suggested that the next phase in the development of what I have called elsewhere [1] the nuclear alliance of Britain, Russia, China, and the United States, is the formation of regional systems: the Atlantic Community, the Russian Orbit, the Chinese Orbit, and later, in a form which I am unable to foresee, Indian and Moslem Communities. In these transformations the wartime alliance of the big powers would be broadened and, I believe, stabilized.

Unless the alliance is victorious, we can, of course, impose no terms on our present enemies. Nor can we settle with them permanently until we know whether

[1] See my *U. S. Foreign Policy*.

the Atlantic Community will hold together and what will be its relations with the Russian Orbit and with the Chinese. The settlement with the vanquished will depend upon the organization of the victors; the conditions they can impose must be determined by the test of how long they can enforce them. What kind of place can be made for Japan and for Germany and offered to their people is a question that can be answered only if there is prior agreement on how the post-war world is to be organized.

1. The Cairo Terms

The Cairo Declaration[2] commits the United States, China, and Great Britain to definite terms which fix new boundaries for Japan. She is to be compelled to return to China all Chinese territory including Manchuria. She is to be ousted from Korea, which "in due course" is to become free and independent. China is to recover the island of Formosa, which Japan conquered in 1895, and also the Pescadores. These provisions achieve the ideal objective of American policy in the Orient, set nearly fifty years ago, to re-establish the territorial integrity of China as it was before the first war waged against her by Japan.

Japan is also to be "stripped of all the islands in the Pacific" which she occupied during the First World War. These are the Carolines, Marshalls, and Marianas, which Japan was allowed to retain in the Versailles set-

[2] December 1, 1943. For text see Appendix X.

tlement of 1919, nominally under mandate from the League of Nations.

Japan will also be ousted from all the territory she has dominated or occupied since the summer of 1940. This means Indo-China, Thailand, Burma, and Malaya in Southeast Asia; the Philippines, the Netherlands Indies, and all the islands of the South Pacific.

Taken as a whole these terms mean that Japan is to be expelled from the Asiatic mainland and is to lose her sea power in the Pacific. Japan becomes once more an island nation. She is to be an island nation near a continent where she has no foothold, and in an ocean which others command.

There would be no point in imposing these terms now if we did not incorporate them in a settlement which would last. It must begin as a settlement which Japan cannot undo; it must become a settlement which the Japanese nation will in the end accept.

This is the general aim of any lasting settlement of a war of aggression: to extinguish the war party and to protect the peace party by making the defeat irrevocable and the peace acceptable.

For Japan the defeat is irrevocable if she cannot return to the mainland of Asia from which she is to be expelled, if she cannot recover command of any part of the Pacific Ocean. Within her own islands, having no military control over, but only commercial access to, the resources and man power of Asia or of the Pacific,

Japan cannot restore her military power. Her three nearest great neighbors — the Soviet Union, America supported by Great Britain, and China as she achieves her development — will be indubitably stronger.

Once Japan is ousted from the mainland, she cannot return without the consent of Russia and China. Once she is ousted from the islands of the Pacific, she cannot return to them if the United States is determined to prevent her. Therefore, the terms defined in the Cairo Declaration will last if Russia, China, and the United States stand firmly upon them.

In order to be clear about the implications of the Japanese settlement, we must then fix our attention on the worst possible eventualities which might arise. When we do this, we see that Japan can escape from the settlement by breaking up the concert of power among China, Russia, and the United States. If these three powers have a serious quarrel, Japan will have the opportunity, and with the opportunity the incentive, to try again.

For if there is a serious quarrel among these three powers, some, and more likely all of them, are certain to make a bid for Japanese support. Japan alone could never fight her way back onto the Asiatic mainland. But Japan, allied with the Soviet Union against China, or with China against the Soviet Union, could be invited back. She could be assisted to recover her military strength, enabled to recover it because she would hold the balance of power among the disunited Allies.

The settlement with Japan is a three-legged stool which

cannot stand if any one of the three powers alters its policy in respect to Japan. Is any one of them likely to alter its policy? All we can say is that the powers would be sacrificing their vital interests to some lesser interest if they altered it. The ejection of Japan from the Asiatic mainland will liberate China. It will give Russia in Siberia a security which she has never before enjoyed. It will give the United States immunity to the challenge of hostile sea power in the whole Pacific. No conflict of vital interest exists. The United States can have no territorial claims in Asia, and no possible interest in blocking the free access of China and Russia to the sea. China and Russia, on the other hand, are vast continental states, and they cannot, without risking too much to gain nothing, entertain the ambition to become amphibious powers in order to challenge the command of the ocean. Russia and China are elephants. We are a whale. Each can rest in its own element. There is no reason why they should fight.

Serious conflict among the three nations can arise on the long borderland between China and Russia, or in liberated Korea, which will be a tender spot because it is a weak spot. Between China proper and the Soviet Union the boundaries are not clearly fixed or well settled. For where Russia and China meet in Asia, both are empires in the sense that they exercise varying degrees of authority over many diverse peoples.[3] We do not

[3] Cf. Carl Becker, *How New Will the Better World Be?* Alfred A. Knopf, New York, 1944, p. 93.

think of China or of Russia as an empire, but, as Becker says: "I suppose that if Siberia, with its eight or ten millions of non-Russian inhabitants . . . were an island or group of islands separated from Russia . . ." or "if Mongolia, Manchuria, Tibet and Sinkiang were scattered about in the Indian Ocean," we should have no difficulty in recognizing that there is a Russian or a Chinese empire in the same sense that there is a British or a French. Between the national state of China and the Soviet Union, there lie Manchuria, Jehol, Sinkiang, the Mongolian People's Republic and the Tannu Tuva People's Republic.[4] There is, moreover, Korea, which is placed in relation to China, Russia, and Japan much as Belgium is to Britain, France, and Germany.

It would be idle to pretend that no trouble is likely to arise upon a borderland of this unsettled character. The question will be whether the vital interest of all these powers will override their inevitable local disputes. The best insurance we can have is to be fully aware that a critical dispute in the Asiatic borderland could rupture the settlement with Japan and precipitate a great war.

[4] *A New Atlas of China*, by Marthe Rajchman, Descriptive Text by the Staff of *Asia Magazine*, with an Introduction by H. E. Yarnell, Rear Admiral, U. S. N. (retired). The John Day Company, New York, 1941, p. 6.

2. The Reform of Japan

Our own greatest interest is to preserve the strategic settlement. Therefore, in the political treatment of the Japanese nation we should all of us, Russia, Britain, America, seek to follow the leadership of China. This is the best way to avert the great peril of Japan's becoming, in the eyes of the whole Oriental world, an Oriental people persecuted by Westerners.

We shall have to assume that the Chinese are better judges than we can hope to be as to where the line is to be drawn between justice that Asia will regard as justice and vengeance that Asia will resent as the White Man's domination. The Chinese should be the judges of Allied policy towards the Emperor, they should be the judges of the length and character of the occupation of Japan, and they should be the principals in carrying out what is decided.[5] If China herself is divided or irresolute, we must stand by until her course is certain. The American objective will have been attained if Japan is incapable of recovering the military force to strike again. The reform and reconstruction of Japan are beyond our ken, and we shall be wise to solidify our relations with China by being in these matters her second.

That the reforms will go deep, that they will revolu-

---

[5] Cf. *Fortune Magazine*, April 1944, "What to Do with Japan?" p. 181. "The proposition that we run post-war Japan has only to be stated, accurately and honestly, to be rejected."

tionize the social and cultural order of Japanese feudal-
ism and imperialism, we must hope. We must stand
ready to give those who come after the war lords a
chance to succeed: by giving the Japanese people a sufficient, though no doubt for some time to come a carefully controlled, access to markets and raw material.
The Japanese must be able to earn a decent living
peaceably.[6]

But we cannot manage a Japanese revolution. The
utmost we can do is to make the revolution certain by
making the defeat irrevocable.

[6] Never again should we become confused by the propaganda of aggression, that Japan must expand by conquest
because she is a "have-not" nation. The Japanese, says Lattimore, "never were nearly as much a 'have-not' nation as a
peaceful and orderly country like Sweden today. The Japanese were a 'have-not' nation only in one sense: that they
could not, out of the resources of their own country, build
up and maintain a navy and army and air force of a size
that could be used only for aggressive purposes. They
were a 'have-not' nation because they demanded the right
to get from other countries the raw materials to set going
their own aggression against those very countries. . . .

"In Japan, just as in Germany, the springs of aggression
were not within the race, but within the social order. The
Japanese have strong survivals of a feudal system of codified
inequalities between social classes. The privileged people
who benefited by the system refused to abolish it, because
of the inconvenience it would have caused them. As an alternative, they launched into aggression in order to force other
people to pay the price of keeping up the expensive and
inefficient social system within Japan." (Owen Lattimore,
op. cit., pp. 12–13.)

CHAPTER X

SETTLEMENT WITH GERMANY

As with Japan so with Germany. The Allies cannot
find any solution until they have first stabilized their
own relations. The German settlement will be as durable
as the connections between the Atlantic Community and
the Russian Orbit.

We ought to have learned something from our first
failure to settle with Germany, and the symbols of that
failure are Versailles, Munich, and the Hitler-Stalin
Pact of August 1939. Under the Versailles Treaty Germany was disarmed. But the enforcement of the disarmament was left to France alone. East of Germany there
was a congeries of small and discordant states committed
to a dual task which was entirely beyond their powers.
They were expected to police Germany. They were also
expected to quarantine Russia. By occupying the Rhineland in 1936 Hitler drove a wedge between France and
her small eastern allies. At Munich he made the small
allies helpless, and isolated them, as well as France and
Britain, from Russia. Then in the Hitler-Stalin Pact of
1939 he obtained a free hand for the assault on the west.

Germany proved her ability to rearm in spite of the

terms of the Versailles Treaty; the primary reason she could do so was because the nations in Europe were suspicious and disunited.

1. Many Questions with One Answer

It is generally agreed this time that Germany must be thoroughly disarmed: the question is who will stand guard, and for how long? Some argue that Germany should lose territory to Poland; but if so, the question is how will Poland defend this territory? Some say that the left bank of the Rhine should be detached from the Reich; then the question is how will France hold it?

Others protest that there should be no annexation of any territory held by Germany before the appearance of Hitler: the question is how the Polish Corridor, the Sudetenland, Austria, the Saar, and Alsace-Lorraine are to be defended more surely after this war than they were defended before this war? Still others demand that Germany be broken up forcibly into two or more Germanies: the question immediately arises of how they are to be prevented from reuniting? Others suggest that while Germany cannot be broken up forcibly, inducements should be offered to parts of Germany to secede and form separate states: the question is who can safely offer the sufficient inducements? Could France, could Poland, could Austria?

It is believed that for a long time to come the foreign commerce and the industrial development of Germany must be subjected to a regime of international control:

the question again is who in fact will administer this control and for how long? It is also said that the Fourth Principle of the Atlantic Charter requires that Germany, though disarmed, be given at once "access, on equal terms, to the trade and the raw materials of the world": the question is how the liberated countries of Europe, which have been ravished and their population deci-mated, are to restore their economic independence if they have to compete with the superior German econ-omy, intact except for physical damage which can soon be repaired?

It is said that there are good Germans and bad Ger-mans. Some argue from this truism that we must support the German democrats, while others point to the record and argue that the German democrats have always fol-lowed the German militarists: the question is can we support the German democrats against the militarists, who will certainly wish to overthrow the democrats as they did the Weimar Republic; or, if the pessimists hap-pen to be right, can we prevent the democrats from fol-lowing the militarists?

To all these questions there is no answer unless we can say with assurance that the nations surrounding Ger-many will be solidly organized, each nation being defi-nitely committed in its own strategical system of security to carrying out the German settlement. In every one of the plans we have mentioned, this is the implied and the indispensable major premise.

If Germany can detach any of her neighbors, and

draw it into a German orbit, not one of the plans, be it hard or soft, can be made to work. Any plan for disarmament, annexations, dismemberment, any plan for internal policing or external international control, or for keeping intact a democratic Germany with equal economic opportunity, would be frustrated if Germany were able to detach, let us say, France from the Atlantic Community or Poland from the Russian Orbit. If any important neighbor of Germany turned away from the existing alliance to become the ally of Germany, it would begin the fateful disruption of all control over Germany. This would mean the overthrow within Germany of all Germans who accepted the peace settlement. The war party would come out from underground to lead the Germans once more.

The paramount question, therefore, concerns the durability of the strategical and political framework within which the settlement with Germany is made.

2. The Crisis of the German Settlement

This is so much the most important question that if it is answered wisely, we shall not find it necessary to answer many of the other dependent questions. The disarmament of Germany, for example, if she surrenders unconditionally, would not be difficult: it was done partially in 1918 and it can be done thoroughly this time. The difficulty is to keep Germany disarmed. It is difficult to do that because after fifteen years or so have elapsed, the memory of this war will be dim in many countries and a new generation will be on the scene which looks forward, not backward.

How can Germany be kept disarmed? We cannot answer this question, I believe, until we have made up our minds how long she must be specially disarmed. There is no use in our imagining that any special regime can be made to last forever. No plan can be workable if it is supposed to last forever. It will be discredited from the beginning because it will seem foolish, and will be abandoned sooner than would be a more definite and limited plan.

My view is that the crisis will come approximately fifteen years after the armistice.[1] If the armistice is made in 1945, then about 1960 Germany will turn either to preparing a new war or to real peace. By that date the new generation of Germans, men now under thirty, will have become the active leaders in German affairs; the survivors of the present ruling class, of which there will be many, will be in their declining years. The crisis will

[1] There is good historical evidence for the view that a post-war period lasts about fifteen years. After Waterloo in 1815 France had a revolution in 1830. "Reconstruction" after our Civil War was finished by 1880. France, defeated in 1870, was again a great European power by the middle eighties. Hitler came to power fifteen years after the armistice of 1918. Russia had recovered from defeat, revolution, civil war, and ostracism, and was again recognized as a great power in the early thirties. Japan turned against her associates in the First World War thirteen years after it ended. Italy broke with her allies about sixteen years after the end of the war.

turn on whether the new generation breaks with the old men of the war party, or follows them, as the Nazis have followed the old pan-Germans. Around about 1960, the Germans will either accept the settlement, and the war party will die out; or they will revolt against the settlement, and the war party will be reborn.

Fifteen years hence, therefore, the wartime alliance — transformed but consolidated — must be intact or the war party will be able to prove to the new generation that another attempt, without Hitler's mistakes, is a glorious opportunity. Fifteen years hence, also, the new generation must see before it the clear alternative of a good life in peace. If at that critical time the Germans are unable to rearm and to destroy the political framework of the settlement, if the renewal of aggression is plainly impossible and the acceptance of peace is not unprofitable, Germany will almost certainly never again be able to set out to conquer the world.

For by 1970 Germany's eastern neighbors in the Russian Orbit will surpass her overwhelmingly in population, and Russia particularly will be no longer inferior in technology. Not only will the German population cease to grow but its composition will change: there will be a rising proportion of old people to young men of military age. On the other hand, the Soviet Union and, to a lesser but still important degree, Poland, Central Europe and the Balkans, will still be growing rapidly, and will have an enormous superiority of men of military age. This great population with its vast natural resources, and now possessed of the whole modern technology, will by 1970 reduce Germany to a power of relatively second rank.[2]

The real object of the total disarmament of Germany is, I believe, to gain time. We need fifteen years to pass the crisis of the post-war period, and ten or fifteen years, when the crisis has been successfully passed, for nature to take her course.

Until the crisis is passed, a special regime is needed to restore the military power of the occupied countries, to consolidate their military systems within the Atlantic Community in the West and within the Russian Orbit in the East, to thwart the German war party and hold in power the Germans who can become disposed to accept the settlement. Life will be hard in a vanquished Germany. The prospects of escape, which the rupture of the framework would at once open up, would make the drudgery of reconstruction seem intolerably dreary. As long as the militarists can offer an escape from the defeat by a resort to force, a peaceable German democracy will fight a losing and what looks like an inglorious and un-German struggle against them.

3. Our Primary Aim

It will surely be agreed that the permanent defeat of the German war party is necessary to the peace of the

[2] Cf. Frank W. Notestein, "Population and Power in Post-War Europe," in *Foreign Affairs*, Vol. 22, No. 3, April 1944, p. 389. Mr. Notestein is the Director of the Office of Population Research at Princeton University.

world. Only if that is accomplished will Europe and the world be made safe against another German war of aggression. Only then can the German democracy have a chance. The settlement must therefore be designed to defeat the war party.

The deep and abiding objective of the German war party is now, and has been for more than a generation, to separate Eastern Europe and Russia from Western Europe and the Americas. The war party means to conquer: the fundamental tactic in any policy of conquest is to divide and conquer. Even if we defeat it again and once more drive it underground, the war party will not disappear as long as there remains a good gambler's chance that Germany can some day isolate any one of its present enemies, and then conquer it or make it a German satellite.

To isolate its intended victims is the cardinal principle of the war party's strategy and diplomacy. It could be shown, I think — though it is outside the scope of this book — that the main reason why the Paris Peace Conference of 1919 was unable to make a lasting peace, in which the League could have flourished, was that it was unable to organize security east of Germany.

The disunity of Eastern Europe was the opportunity of the German war party: it was the compelling reason why they did not have to accept as final the military defeat of 1918, and the plan of this second German war was laid down almost immediately after the first German war. It was carefully calculated to exploit the weakness which resulted from the isolation of Russia, of Poland, of Czechoslovakia, of Austria, each from all the others. This plan was carried out. The stage was set for this war, and for the great German successes of 1939–1941, by the shrewd and skillful isolation of the victims. The occupation of the Rhineland in 1936 separated France from her discordant allies in Eastern Europe. The occupation of Austria in March 1938 isolated Czechoslovakia for its liquidation, at Munich in September 1938, as a military state. By this Poland was enveloped. By the failure of Poland, Britain, France, and Russia, to unite for the defense of Poland, the Germans isolated Poland. By the 1939 pact between Hitler and Stalin, France was isolated from any possibility of Russian aid. The fall of France isolated Britain. The isolation of Britain laid Russia open in 1941 to invasion by the whole land force of Germany, there being no second front that Germany had to hold.

At enormous cost and danger Germany has been stopped from winning this war by the formation of the alliance which, if it had existed before, could have prevented the war. When the Germans are forced to surrender, their view of the settlement will be determined by whether they believe they can rupture this alliance. If they think they can, the war party will regard the military defeat as a temporary reverse. If they think they cannot, a pacific German democracy may be able to hold down and, in the end, to liquidate the war party.

The terms of peace — which have to do with territory,

disarmament, control, restitution, and the punishment of war criminals — are, of course, immensely important. And they will need to be considered in the light not only of their immediate but of their longer consequences. But I hold that in regard to them, as in regard to the political treatment of Japan, the United States should not take the leading part. As it is best to let the Chinese be our political mentors in the treatment of internal Japanese affairs, so we shall be wise if we let the European peoples, who are the victims of Germany and must yet live next to Germany, settle the moral and the political accounts. We have not had their experience, and we should not make again President Wilson's mistake of imposing our own doctrinaire views on them. They have felt the German aggression. We have only been told about it. They must take the practical consequences of the reckoning with Germany. They must live next to the Germans. Let Germany be judged by her peers. We are too far away to judge wisely and well. For us the paramount consideration is that the settlement shall be durable, and the great question there is whether or not the war party survives in Germany. If it survives, it will be because the Allies give it reason to hope that they can again be duped, separated, and isolated.

The armistice will not finish the war party; it can survive underground for some years, reappearing only in disguise. Its policy will be an adaptation under the new circumstances of its old policy. The outlines of it are already apparent.

If the militarists see any chance of succeeding, they will try to insinuate Germany into the position of holding the balance of power between Russia and the Western World. They will appeal to the Atlantic Community for permission to restore German power in order to balance the might of Russia and check the spread of communism. Whatever success the Germans have with this appeal in Paris, London, and Washington, their diplomats will then use in Moscow. They will use it in order to rouse the old fears of the Soviet Union, that the whole world is arrayed against them as it was in 1919–1921. The Germans will thus try to provoke the Russians to take measures which would then again alienate the Atlantic Community from them.

To the Atlantic Community the Germans would offer anti-bolshevism; to Russia they would offer some new version of the Hitler-Stalin Pact. Their purpose being to disorganize the peace settlement, they would as a matter of course be anti-bolshevist in the West and anti-capitalist in the East. First by grasping, then by holding, the balance of power, they would squirm free of the settlement and begin to rebuild their own military power.

Our primary war aim must be unalterable: it must be to make it as impossible for Germany to hold the balance of power in Europe as for Japan to hold it in Eastern Asia.

This must be our aim even if we take the most pessimistic view of our future relations with Russia. For if we committed ourselves to a policy of restoring German military power as a means of checking Russia, the Russian reaction would be obvious. It would be devastating. Russia could take Germany into her camp much more quickly than we could take Germany into ours. There are ideological differences between national socialism and communism, the critical difference being the Hitlerian doctrine that the Germans are the master race. But shorn of the racist doctrine by the destruction of the nazi leaders — with the *Junker* class, the higher military caste, and the big industrialists liquidated by a revolution that was supported and guided from Russia — National Socialist Germany could rather easily become Soviet Germany.

In a competition to take Germany into camp, the British and French have little, and we have almost nothing, to offer which compares with what the Russians can offer. They can offer Germany a place second only to themselves, and in the whole of Western Europe this would make Germany dominant.

A German-Russian combination would soon become a German-Russian-Japanese combination. For if once the fatal step of seeking alliances with our present enemies were taken by any of the Allies, Russia could much more easily than we take all the other steps.

4. Germany's Place in the Sun

If, as we have seen, our vital interests require a settlement by which Germany cannot become the bone of contention between Russia and the Atlantic States, how can we organize it?

The master clue to such a settlement is not a state secret. It stands out as a principle clear as daylight. It is that the foreign relations of every state should be definitely fixed and not suddenly alterable. That is why we must have the Atlantic Community and the Russian Orbit to make solid the framework of the settlement. The evil for which the various United Nations must find the cure, or Germany will exploit the evil, is a fluctuating, vacillating, erratic foreign policy which causes uncertainty, tension, intrigue, insecurity. We cannot have an order into which Germany can be fitted if we do not cure this evil.

We have anticipated what Germany could and would do if she were allowed to hold the balance of power. It follows that the fundamental condition of a lasting settlement with Germany is to agree upon a definite place which she shall occupy in international society. This place must conform to the vital interests of her neighbors and it must be acceptable eventually, because it is viable, to the German people. For though we are the mortal enemies of their present rulers and the sworn enemies of their whole doctrine and policy of domination, the settlement which we shall make must aim at the long future. Its final purpose must be peace not only in our time but also for our children.

No passion of war can make us wholly forget that the structure of the peace we make now must be one in which the Germans, if they cease to rebel against civilization, will have their place. No such settlement can be acceptable to the German war party. What we are seeking is a peace which Germans who have forever renounced the war party can find appropriate for their genius, and which they can make adequate for their needs. For we cannot wish to police the Germans forever. We must seek a solution in which they will voluntarily observe the law.

In the end, it seems to me, a disarmed Germany can come safely and properly to rest within the international exchange economy of the Atlantic Community. But Germany can be so placed only with the sincere consent of the Soviet Union. Therefore, there must be no question of Germany's being included in the military system of the Atlantic powers. By making a demilitarized Germany dependent on sea-borne commerce, the best guaranty will be provided that the age-long German expansion to the east, the *Drang nach Osten*, is ended.

To end it conclusively and forever, the strategic security of the Russian Orbit will then have to be reinsured by firm alliances between Russia and the other eastern neighbors of Germany. If the borderland between Germany and Russia is a diplomatic no man's land, the small states within it cannot hope to be independent and secure, and no settlement can be made with Germany that Russia as well as the Western nations will agree on.

The organization of this Eastern regional system is the guaranty Russia is bound to take against a third German invasion in this century, and against any sort of anti-

Russian combination by the Western states. It is, moreover, a real guaranty. For it places Russia, which will now surpass Germany as a military power, in a position to prevent the revival of Germany's military power. It is the one sure guaranty that can be given to Russia that no Western country will seek to revive German power for use against Russia. For the Soviet Union will be there to prevent it.

We have to look at these things as the most pessimistic and suspicious Russian might see them if we are to reach conclusions that are solid and sound. Now if Germany is by these means rendered innocuous to Russia, she will also be innocuous to the Atlantic Community. On that foundation of reciprocal security, it will then be clear to Russia why it is her interest as well as ours, and also Germany's, that for a German democracy, neutralized as a military power, a place should be reserved within the Atlantic Community.

There is no other place for a peaceable Germany. For Germany must have a place somewhere. The German people cannot live a self-contained economic life within their frontiers. They will either expand overland in Europe, or they must be allowed to live by trading overseas, by being accepted into the oceanic international exchange economy.

German economic expansion in Europe means German militarism and pan-German domination; this war is being waged to exterminate both. It will be safer for all of Europe, and also for Russia, if Germany becomes dependent upon maritime commerce. The less self-sufficient Germany is, the better for her neighbors whom she has sought to dominate, and for the Atlantic nations which will emerge from this war with the command of the seas.

This does not mean that the Germans can or should be given a free run in the markets of the world. Not until the period of probation is over, and there have been radical changes in their way of doing business, can German trade pass unregulated. But it does mean that a trade, which the Allies regulate and supervise as to its amount, its origins, its destination, and its terms, should be developed between Germany and parts of the extra-European world. It might well be that for the probation period German nationals should not be permitted to have business agencies abroad because they are known to be the foci of political conspiracy and propaganda. It might even be that Germans should do their international trading only at German ports, and beyond them through Allied agencies. These are, relatively speaking, details. The main point at the moment is that within Germany an important part of the working population should manufacture for non-European markets in payment for imports from overseas.

This conclusion will at first be unpalatable to the Western countries which would have to receive Germany into their trading community; it may well be highly suspect to the Russians on the ground that it extends the political influence of the Western states to the very frontiers of their strategic neighborhood. Yet these first reactions must be weighed against the alternatives.

The permanent isolation of Germany is not a solution of the German problem. The attempt to isolate Germany will surely fail if it is extended beyond the time when her victims, and the Germans who now oppress them, are still in active life. The peoples of the world simply will not spend many long years supervising Germany in a reform school. Eventually Germany must have a recognized place of her own in the scheme of things. The real alternatives are a place in the Atlantic Community or in the Russian Orbit.

But in the Russian Orbit there is no place for Germany which is safe and tolerable for the Eastern states or for the Western. A Germany integrated with Russia would be a dangerous and menacing internal enemy of the Soviet Union. The very essence of pan-Germanism, which is German infiltration and domination to the east, would remain in the form of a subversive movement within the Russian Orbit. Moreover, a Germany facing east would be a crushing weight upon the political and economic life of the border nations from Poland to the Danubian countries and the Balkans. And as the inclusion of Germany within the Russian Orbit would bring it to the shores of the Atlantic, this solution would be intolerable for the Western World.

But as a demilitarized trading nation within the Atlantic Community, Germany would be made as safe as it is possible to make her for Europe and for the world.

5. The Mirage of European Federation

There are many who will dislike this settlement because they would prefer a European federation which might be called the United States of Europe. This noble project has a long history: "Since the fourteenth century," says Ross Hoffman, "the idea of bringing the states to federation has been in the European mind. As early as 1307 the French *légiste* Pierre Dubois had drafted a scheme for forming a union of Christian nations under the lead of the King of France." [3] At the end of the sixteenth century Henry Fourth's minister, Sully, set forth a comprehensive plan: "Europe would be composed of fifteen dominions nearly equal in size and strength and these would be constitutionally integrated in a permanent league." The proposal was adapted to the needs of the eighteenth century by the Abbé de Saint-Pierre. After the War of the Spanish Succession, which ended in 1714, he proposed to form "a permanent league of European states on the basis of the status quo; which league would command an international army and have power to enforce submission to its collective will." After the Napoleonic Wars these ideas influenced the conception of the Holy Alliance, and after the First World War they were revived by Aristide Briand.

The idea has persisted so long because there are in fact a culture and a tradition of which all good Europeans, despite national differences, are profoundly conscious.

[3] Ross Hoffman, *op. cit.*

This gives them the rudiments of a common European patriotism and the conviction, in Mr. Churchill's words,[4] that "thus and thus only will the glory of Europe rise again."

I do not believe that the ideas developed in this book run counter to this great project of unity. If I did, I too should shrink away from them. For it is through Europe that the threads connecting the Americas and Eurasia will have to be woven together. But I believe that the political federation of Europe will not serve this great end, and that in our time certainly it would be a great evil.

I base my argument upon the fact that while Europe is the seat of a culture which has spread over large portions of the earth, Europe is not a geographic and strategic entity which can be organized as a political federation. For what would the boundaries of this federation be? Which nations does the United States of Europe exclude and which does it include?

The main sponsor of the project in this country is an organization called the Pan-European Conference. It proposes the immediate political federation of Europe with one central government from Portugal to Poland, and from Scandinavia to Greece and Italy inclusive. Is this a desirable project for this country to espouse? Its partisans often imply that regional systems are evil

[4] His speech of March 21, 1943. We may note that Mr. Churchill did not propose the *political* federation of Europe at the end of this war.

things and that theirs is a more constructive plan. But in fact a politically federated Europe is also a regional system. The question is not whether there should or should not be regional systems in the world. It is whether continental Europe should form a separate regional system.

If it does, can there be any doubt that Germany would be the hard core of the European federation? Germany would hold the strategic center of the federation, would be the strongest military state within it and the main arsenal: would not the Germans, as the most highly disciplined people on the Continent, dominate the federation as Prussia dominated the federal German Reich after 1871? No blueprint can provide against the very nature of things in Europe.

The Pan-European Conference calls the proposed European army by the euphemistic name of "the Federal Police Force." The European army is to be composed of professional soldiers, not more than 10 per cent of its effectives are to come from any one European nation, and its commander-in-chief is to be chosen from a small nation. For my own part I cannot see how the Swiss, the Danish, or the Belgian commander-in-chief is to get around the fact that the German 10 per cent of the effectives, rightly placed in the general staff and the commands, would be the cadre of the new European army. The Germans are indisputably the greatest military people on the Continent: no other European state has a comparable body of seasoned soldiers. Seventy thousand Germans were employed to train the Soviet Army of the 1920's; they became the core of the present German Army. In 1944 our old regular army is probably not so much as 5 per cent of the effectives: but the old army is the core of the new one. The Germans would be the core of any European army, or police force if that is the word for it. Besides the professional police force, which alone "controls mechanized weapons," there are to be, say the advocates of European federation, "national forces" which act only as "local militias." How are the militias of France, Poland, or the Netherlands to be equipped? It is proposed that "the entire armament industry and traffic" of the Continent "should become a federal monopoly." Now the fact is that much the greater part of that monopoly is physically within Germany and would be managed by Germans.

The conclusion is inescapable, it seems to me, that if we espouse now the political federation of the European Continent, we shall make the Continent a regional system dominated by Germany. This is precisely what the war is being fought to prevent. I realize that those who favor political federation do not want a German Europe. But a German Europe is just what they would get. They would get it because they have not seen that Europe must be made secure against Germany, which has twice tried to conquer it, before Europe can safely be federated.

Europe as such is not strong enough to withstand German domination. It has needed, and until Germany is transformed it will need, the military power of Great Britain, Russia, and America to insure its security. Now the military force of these three non-European powers cannot be made available to check the German war party if the military plan of European defense is organized from Germany and *against* them rather than around Germany and *by* them. If Great Britain and the United States are to support France and Western Europe, the military system of Western Europe must be co-ordinated with theirs. The political federation of Europe would co-ordinate it with Germany. If the Soviet Union is to check Germany from the east, the military system of the central and eastern European states must be co-ordinated not with Germany but with Russia.

Only when Europe is secure against German domination can the unity of Europe be made consistent with the independence and freedom of the non-German nations. It is on the foundation of security, which is obtainable by forming the Atlantic Community and the Russian Orbit, that an economic and cultural federation is possible. Then it will be highly desirable. Then the other agencies of government that are concerned with commerce and welfare can and should bind the civilian life of the Continent together in matters affecting tariffs, commercial policy, money, transportation, public utilities, social security, and the like. These are matters for Europeans to deal with.

But at the end of this war *our* first war aims must be concerned with how the war-making powers, the military forces, and the diplomacy which sets them in motion, are distributed and aligned.

PART FOUR

A Long Peace or the Third World War

CHAPTER XI

U.S.S.R. AND U.S.A.

By THE wise use of our victory we can now put an end
to the series of wars which have devastated the world
for some thirty years. We can then have something
much better than another armistice which will last only
as long as the nations are too weary to fight again. We
can have a long peace such as no man now of middle age
has ever known. We can come again into a time when
wars and the rumors of wars are not our constant and
terrible preoccupation. We shall have earned the great
chance to turn again from the struggle for existence to
the pursuit of happiness and the good life.

Whether we meanly lose or nobly seize this golden
opportunity will depend on whether we can pierce
through the smoke and dust of the struggle and see that
an unfinished but nevertheless great structure of peace
and order has already been raised from the ruins. In
order to win the war the nations have had to draw together, finding their places within the scheme of things.
This *is* the new world order. If we preserve it and en-
hance it, we shall inaugurate a long peace. If we ignore
it and wreck it, we must prepare for another series of
great wars.

More than upon anything else the outcome depends upon the relations between the Soviet Union and the United States. Each is now the center of gravity within vast areas of the earth. They can prevent a third World War. If they fight, it will be the most terrible of all world wars.

Never before in modern times has there been such a distribution of military force as will obtain when this war is won. The two strongest states in the world will be as widely separated as it is possible to be: the core of the Soviet power is at the Urals in the deep interior of the Eurasian continent; the American power is in the Mississippi Valley in the heart of the island continent of North America. Not since the unity of the ancient world was disrupted has there been so good a prospect of a settled peace. Before the division of the Mediterranean World, there was such a wide separation between the Roman power and the powers in Asia that for some centuries there was no great struggle for survival.

We have come again to an age when the two leading powers capable of waging great war are, as respects one another, invulnerable.

1. Preface to a Russian Policy

If we are to stabilize our relations with the Soviet Union, we must study its vital interests and our own, and establish a policy accordingly. But we must recognize at the outset that in the Western nations there are profound differences of opinion as to Russia's interests and intentions. There are those who hold that the Russians will for a long time to come be absorbed in the internal development of their vast country, and that the Soviet Union will be very nearly as self-centered as was the United States during the nineteenth century. This is one hypothesis. There is no way of proving that it is correct.

The other view is, of course, that Soviet Russia is an aggressive state which in various combinations fuses the ambitions of the Czarist Empire with the projects of the Third International. There is no way of proving that this hypothesis is incorrect.

But a foreign policy ought not to be based on a blind choice between two unprovable hypotheses. We need to be prepared for all the eventualities that can reasonably be anticipated. This is the elementary rule of prudence in statecraft — which is to work for the best that is possible and to be prepared for the worst that may happen.

For this reason, whatever may be our private guesses, I hold that our true policy with Russia does not require us to prejudge the question of whether Russia is to be a dynamic expanding power or a satisfied and quiet one. On either hypothesis, or any variation between extreme optimism and extreme pessimism, we shall serve our vital interests by maintaining and perfecting the Atlantic Community. For if the worst that men fear is going to happen, it will be upon the solidarity of Western Europe and the Americas that we shall have to rely. This solidarity is our ultimate insurance. But it is also the best possible foundation upon which to work for good relations with the Soviet Union. For in the last analysis nothing is so certain to promote the will to keep the peace as the certainty that nothing could be decided and nothing could be gained by war.

2. *The Elephant and the Whale*

A Russian-American war is, as such, a virtual impossibility. In the West the two countries cannot get at one another except by crossing Europe. They might wage border warfare where Siberia and Alaska meet. But Americans could not invade and occupy the Urals by way of Alaska, nor Russians the Mississippi Valley by way of Siberia. No competent soldier would contemplate seriously either project.

Aerial bombing across the Arctic will no doubt become technically feasible in the near future. But only uncritical speculation can suppose that air forces based on Russian and on American soil could in the foreseeable future be capable of deciding a Russian-American conflict. The notion is quite contrary to all technological experience: it assumes that while the offensive power of the bomber will grow without limits, the anti-aircraft defense will not grow correspondingly. In the foreseeable future, which is all that statesmen can deal with, a war waged directly between Russia and the United States is very nearly as impossible as a battle between an elephant and a whale.

War is possible, however, if it is a general war in which

the other nations participate. This is the reality with which we must be concerned. Russia and the United States can fight one another in the East if Japan and China provide the striking points, the battlefields, the bridgeheads, the covering forces of the defense, the advanced echelons of the assault. They can fight one another in the West if all of Europe and Great Britain are involved first. Only by means of allies can Russia and the United States come to grips; and by a conflict begun among their allies they can be entangled in a war.

Thus Russia and America are in the position where the issue of war and peace between them will be determined by the policy they follow in respect to their alliances. I am using the word "alliance" to cover any agreement among governments, whether it be formal or informal, avowed or implicit, that makes them partners in the event of war. Russia and America can have peace if they use their alliances to stabilize the foreign policy of their allies. They will have war if either of them reaches out for allies within the orbit of the other, and if either of them seeks to incorporate Germany or Japan within its own strategical system. The whole world would know at once that the preliminaries of the third World War had occurred if the Soviet Union made an alliance with Germany, with Japan, or a separate and exclusive alliance with any member of the Atlantic Community.[1] Equally, if the Atlantic Com-

---

[1] The British-Soviet twenty-year mutual assistance agreement (May 26, 1942) is not separate or exclusive. Cf. Article 3.

munity, or any individual member of it, say Great Britain or France, made an alliance — which was not open to the Soviet Union or not made with its consent — with Germany, or with any state within the Russian Orbit, say Poland, the event would be the certain sign that the structure of the peace had been fatally broken.

3. A Test of Aggression

By recognizing the principle of regional grouping we come upon a practical working rule for discerning aggression. If war is to be prevented, aggression must be checked long before the aggressor crosses a frontier and commits what is known as an overt act. To wait that long is to give the aggressor all the advantages of the initiative and surprise; and a system of collective security which goes into action only when the overt act has been committed cannot *prevent* war. It can only wage war under conditions and at a moment which best suit the aggressor. The time when war can be prevented is before the aggressor is able to strike. That time is when he makes the first diplomatic move to isolate his victim.

Under the regional principle which I am advocating, it would be held to be an overt act of aggression for any state to reach out beyond its own strategical orbit for an alliance with a state in another orbit. Within the same strategical neighborhood alliances are good: neighbors must and should combine for their common security. But alliances are bad if they disrupt the solidarity of a neighborhood; they are entangling and interventionist if they bring an alien power into the midst of a neighborhood. No one questions our alliances with Canada and Mexico. But if Mexico made an alliance with the Soviet Union, everyone would know at once that the peace was troubled. If we made an alliance with Iran or with Romania, all the world would have every right to think the worst of our intentions.

This rule of conduct can be administered and enforced. For the compacts under which the members of a regional system, such as the Atlantic Community, organized their military forces would be bound to provide, as a matter of right and duty, for access to information about their military establishments, for full disclosure, and for continuing consultation in their military planning. Under these circumstances no member of the community could make an effective secret military alliance. The mere withholding of information would be a warning signal that something disloyal was contemplated. For while diplomats might conceal a document, they could not conceal a rearrangement of their armies, and the very effort to conceal military information would at once be apparent to the intelligence officers among their allies.

In the days to come the regional principle will be natural and self-evident because the two strongest world powers, Russia and America, are so far apart. Moreover, now and in the future we can foresee, the disparity in power between the greatest states and all others will be wider than it has ever been. Military technology has brought this about: no state smaller than the greatest can hope to match, or even to make a good stand against, the mechanized armies, the air power, and the amphibious armadas of the greatest military states. We can entertain no illusions about this. In a conflict between two great powers equally prepared for war, the modern offensive weapons may be neutralized by the defensive weapons, and the issue decided finally by the infantry. But in a conflict between a great power and one of even second rank, the superiority of the modern offensive weapons is overwhelming. It is so overwhelming that it is not only useless but positively dangerous for a smaller state to attempt to isolate itself by organizing military defenses against a great neighbor. If it does not become the ally of its great neighbor, finding security within the protective power of the great state, it will in time of war become a battlefield where the great powers fight.

The regional grouping of states in combined strategical systems is, therefore, indispensable to the general security of great and small nations alike, and to the stabilization of the relations among states.

4. The Inequality of Intercourse between U.S.S.R. and U.S.A.

There is little doubt that regional grouping will do much to stabilize relations between the Soviet Union and the United States. It provides the security which must be the primary aim of each country. It provides each with a means of recognizing aggression. On this stable foundation the other questions which will affect the relations between the two countries can be approached without fear and with a candor that would not otherwise be possible. Since our relations with the Soviet Union will determine whether there is to be a Third World War, our Russian policy must be not for a summer's day alone: it must be made stout and be battened down to withstand the storms of winter.

The Soviet Union's relations with the United States, and indeed with all other European and American countries, are beset by profound contradictions which inhibit confident collaboration. We encounter them first in the fact that diplomatic intercourse is not on an equal and reciprocal basis. The Soviet government maintains a quarantine against free intercourse with us. The outgoing censorship permits us to know about Russia only what the government deems expedient. The incoming censorship permits the Russian people to know about us, even about our official acts, only what the Soviet government deems expedient. Within the United States citizens may oppose the Administration on a policy dealing with Russia, and if they can muster enough popular support, the policy, or even the Administration, can be changed. But on a Soviet policy towards the United States there is no appeal from the decisions of the government.

The Soviet quarantine means that in foreign affairs the

Soviet government can use secrecy and surprise to maneuver in ways which democratic governments cannot do. Our institutions are such that we could not, without destroying them, equalize intercourse by establishing our own quarantine. Unlike the Soviet's, our policies can be formed only after deliberation and debate which put the whole world on notice.

The Soviet Union does not tolerate the existence of any opposition party which could become the government. But we not only recognize opposition parties as inherent and necessary to our constitutional system; we also tolerate an opposition party, namely the communist, which if it gained power and followed the Soviet model would abolish all parties opposing it and establish the totalitarian rule of the one-party system. Thus, while Russia has insulated herself internally against the propaganda of the Western constitutional system, we are not insulated, because of our principles of toleration, against the totalitarian propaganda. The phenomenon of red-baiting has its roots in this inequality and disparity. It is a convulsive, instinctive, and often neurotic reaction of fear and inferiority in the presence of the fact that while the Soviet constitution is protected by its police against being subverted by democrats, the democracies are inhibited by their own principles from protecting themselves conclusively against being subverted by totalitarians.

As long as this inequality exists, there cannot be true collaboration between the Soviet Union and the Western

World. There can be only a *modus vivendi*, only compromises, bargains, specific agreements, only a diplomacy of checks and counter-checks.

5. The Vicious Circle of Antagonism

After this initial difficulty we come to another. In recent times, certainly since 1941, Soviet foreign policy has disavowed the project of revolutionary international communism and has professed full support of democratic institutions and principles abroad. The Soviet Constitution of 1936 is democratic in character and contains a bill of civil rights; these democratic provisions of the constitution have never yet been made operative in Soviet Russia. It is inevitable then that the world should ask whether the new democratic professions of Soviet foreign policy will in fact be operative. We cannot gloss over this matter if our object is to come to full understanding with Soviet Russia. Too much is at stake, a long peace of collaboration or a third World War. We have to grasp the nettle firmly. The world order in the coming generation will rest jointly upon the Atlantic Community and the Soviet Union. It cannot command the confidence and loyalty of the peoples of the world if this ideological conflict over the elemental civil rights of man is not resolved.

But before we can with sincerity and a good conscience discuss this question, let us remind ourselves of the other side of the coin. Russia has not forgotten that at the close of the First World War, her former allies, while proclaiming the ideals of non-interference and non-intervention, sent troops into Russia to participate in the civil war. Russia's distrust of the Western Powers, which is the counterpart of their distrust of Russia, can be finally overcome by our support of a peace settlement which ends conclusively the German and Japanese threat to Russia's security. On that foundation we can then proceed to seek boldly a durable understanding with the Soviet Union.

The conflict over elemental civil rights, which is the root of the difficulty, can be resolved, and we have the right to hope that it will be. Since we became allies in war, the Soviet Union has been committing itself more and more definitively to a foreign policy based on democratic, and not totalitarian, principles. The differences which have arisen over the application of these principles to concrete cases, chiefly as regards Poland, would not be so stubborn if it were not for the profound doubt as to whether the Soviet Union, which has not yet put its own liberal constitution into effect at home, can be counted upon to remain true to its democratic professions abroad.

Yet the fact is that Marshal Stalin has now repeatedly affirmed the democratic principle in respect to his dealings with his neighbors within the Russian Orbit. In the agreement for "mutual assistance and post-war collaboration" with the Czechoslovak Republic,[2] the Soviet Union has subscribed to "the principles of mutual respect of their independence and sovereignty as well as non-

[2] Signed in Moscow, December 12, 1943.

interference in the internal affairs of the other state." A
protocol to this agreement offers to make the same agreement with "any third power bordering on the U.S.S.R.
or the Czechoslovak Republic, and representing in this
war an object of German aggression." Poland and
Austria fit these specifications. Poland is also specifically
covered by Stalin's statements of May 4, 1943, and
Austria by the Declaration on Austria made at the Tripartite Conference in Moscow, November 1, 1943. Romania has been covered by Molotov's statement of
April 2, 1944, and Finland is covered by the armistice
terms offered her on February 16, 1944. Moreover in
principle and by analogy all enemy and satellite states
are covered by the formal agreement, signed by the
Soviet Union at Moscow and known as the "Declaration
regarding Italy." [3]

This impressive series of agreements and declarations
was made by the Soviet Union after the tide of battle
had turned in favor of the Red Army. Making all possible discounts, they at least express the policy with
which the Soviet government wished to be identified in
the eyes of its allies, and of the occupied and satellite
countries, at a time when Russia was no longer on the
defensive, was in fact carrying successfully the main
burden of the offensive against Germany, and had every
prospect of being the predominant military power of
the Eurasian continent.

These official documents commit the Russians to sup-

[3] Appendix VIII.

port democratic institutions abroad, they commit them against totalitarian institutions outside of the legal frontiers of the Soviet Union. Thus the formal position, publicly avowed and subscribed to, is that even in Eastern Europe and the Balkans, which are within the Russian strategical orbit, the Soviet Union will not interfere in the internal affairs of states, will not promote or support communist parties, factions, or propaganda. Now the Soviet government has total control over the acts of all persons within its borders. So its declarations of non-interference must be construed to cover the acts not only of the Soviet government but of Soviet citizens and of committees of foreigners within the Soviet jurisdiction.

But the declarations say also that the Soviet policy is, in the words of the one about Italy, "based upon the fundamental principle that fascism and all its evil influence and configuration shall be completely destroyed." We are signers of this same declaration, and are of course committed by it. The crux of the difficulty, and the seeds of trouble in the future, is how to reach an understanding on what is necessary to destroy fascism. Measures which Russia deems necessary to destroy fascism may elsewhere be interpreted as measures to promote communism; measures which non-Soviet states may regard as a proper defense against communism may be interpreted in Russia as the support of fascism.

We know how the fear of bolshevism causes some men to become fascists, or at least to tolerate them on the supposition that they are the lesser of two evils. And we know how the fear of fascism causes other men to become communists, or at least to become fellow travelers, looking for allies who are the foes of their foes. It is a vicious circle. In the vital interest of the Russian people, as in our own, we must break this vicious circle. Otherwise the Russians — fighting fascism as they define it — and the Westerners — fighting communism as they define it — may end up as mortal enemies in a world war.

This could happen. Since this could happen, we must deal with it as if it were going to happen. Whatever our sympathies and opinions happen to be, we must not pull the bedcovers over our heads, hoping that if we do not hear too much about the ideological conflict it will somehow subside. We must resolve this conflict in order to make possible a settlement of the war in which men will have confidence, and find tranquillity. We must resolve it in order to extinguish the smoldering coals which may otherwise set the world on fire.

By the candor and boldness of our policy, we may be able to do this.

6. The Radical Solution

We do not have to argue with the Soviets as to whether democratic principles or the revolutionary and totalitarian are to prevail. They themselves have proclaimed their adherence to democratic principles not only by these recent declarations of foreign policy but by the new constitution which they adopted in 1936. The ideological conflict, which matters only as it pertains to elementary human rights, does not in theory exist. In fact it does exist because the Soviet constitution has never yet been put fully into effect.

We may admit at once that in almost all other countries there are differences, often wide and glaring differences, between what they say and do at home and what they do and say abroad. But in the West when practice does not correspond with principle, or when there is a double standard of morality — one for use abroad and one for use at home — we can be charged, and indeed we do charge ourselves in free discussion, with violating our principles or with hypocrisy.

No such charge is made by Russians in Russia, and the world is left to guess why, despite her constitution, the Soviet Union is still in fact a totalitarian state under the dictatorship of the Communist Party. Those who are well-disposed towards Russia can say with Sorokin that "the stern regime" now prevailing is no longer the communist terror and unlimited dictatorship of the early revolutionary period of 1918–1922, but is a "regime of martial law" arising out of "national necessity" in face of the nazi aggression.[4] Those who are fearful or ill-

---

[4] P. A. Sorokin, *Russia and the U. S.* E. P. Dutton & Company, Inc., New York, 1944, pp. 131–139. Professor Sorokin of Harvard University was imprisoned three times by the Czar and twice by the Soviets — always for opposition to the existing regime.

disposed will say that in professing the democratic ideology, while practising dictatorship, the Soviet government is acting in bad faith for the purpose of deceiving and ruling mankind.

Good and confident relations cannot be established by arguing which of these interpretations is the right one. Only the Soviets — not foreign observers — can settle the argument once and for all by what they do when the war is over, and even as the war proceeds, to make their own constitution operative. For what is the world to make of it if they do not?

The earlier, the 1924, constitution of the U.S.S.R. said in its opening declaration (Section I) that "the states of the world have divided into two camps — that of capitalism and that of socialism." This was said, of course, before the Soviet leaders had foreseen that there would be a third camp of fascism and nazism, the camp with which Russia is now at war. The Russian constitution of the pre-fascist period declared that "the very structure of the Soviet power, which is international in its class character, calls the working masses of the Soviet Republics toward a unity of one socialist family . . ." that "admission to this Union shall be open to all Socialist Soviet Republics," and that the "new united state . . . shall . . . form a decisive step towards the Union of the workers of all countries into one World Socialist Soviet Republic." The Communist, or Third, International existed to promote this World Socialist Soviet Republic. Thus in 1928 it declared that "the Red Army is not an 'enemy' army but the army of the international proletariat." [5]

This is the Soviet Russia which the democratic nations feared, and they are still fearful that this may be the true face of Soviet Russia. This fear has not been removed, among many it has been sharpened, by the fact that the *new* Soviet constitution, which was adopted in 1936, contains (in Chapter X) a complete and, indeed, an expanded, bill of rights, and also (in Chapter XI) an electoral system "on the basis of universal, equal and direct suffrage by direct ballot." For in the eyes of many this seems to be calculated deception.

We owe it to the Soviet people to say that however correct may be our diplomatic relations, they will not really be the good relations they need to be until the basic political and human liberties are established in the Soviet Union. Only then will there be full confidence, and a free intercourse on a basis of full equality. For between states that do not have free institutions and those that do have them, international relations must necessarily be special and restricted.

A world order under the reign of universal laws cannot be realized under these conditions. Without the full collaboration of the Soviet Union no universal society can be formed. For in all the critical areas of the world

[5] From the theses advanced at the Sixth Congress of the Communist International, 1928. (T. A. Taracouzio, *The Soviet Union and International Law.* The Macmillan Company, New York, 1935, p. 445.)

— critical with reference to a long peace or a third World War — the Soviet Union is a principal power. In Europe it is the nearest of the great powers to Germany. In Eastern Asia it is the nearest to China and Japan. In the Middle East it is potentially the nearest and most powerful neighbor of the emergent Moslem states. Second only to China, it is substantially the nearest to India. In the universal society, which the Moscow and Teheran agreements call for, there cannot be genuine consultation and, after deliberation, common action, if between the Soviet Union and the other nations there is not an equal and reciprocal exchange of public information, if all the governments which wield force are not publicly accountable to their peoples and to the opinions of the world. The world order cannot be half democratic and half totalitarian.

The wartime association can be maintained for a while until the nations recover from exhaustion, but not for long after that. It will break up into unfriendly blocs unless the regional groups cohere into a world order in which they collaborate. It would be far better not to found a world order than to found one which cannot succeed and yet raises false hopes. We must not have another League of Nations that fails.

If the world order is to be able to succeed, its active and controlling members must be capable of true collaboration. Therefore, in the drafting of its constitution, we should, I believe, propose the inclusion in it of a bill of rights for the member states. The bill should be those

civil rights which are common to the Soviet constitution
and to the constitutions of all Western states. There are
in every country rights which are peculiar to that country. But there are rights which are recognized in all of
these constitutions, and these may be regarded as the
elementary and universal rights of man.

To incorporate a bill of rights in the constitutional
charter of the world society would, of course, be a pledge
to make this bill of rights operative. The Soviet Union
would be bound to put its own constitution into effect:
the Western democracies would be bound to maintain
their constitutional systems, as against totalitarian movements, fascist or communist. All would be bound to support one another — to give no aid and comfort to subversive parties, to approve their suppression,[6] to recognize
no totalitarian government and to quarantine it.

The world society would thus become the protector
and active champion of democracy and freedom. If it is
not that, it will be a mere mechanism and procedure,
divorced from the vital realities of the world, and without a living faith which enlists the devotion of mankind.
It will be a mere forum for contention, an arena of conflict and maneuver.

So we must go to the Russians; the key to the door is
in their hands. Speaking to them frankly as allies who
mean to be their friends, we must ask them to commit

[6] As has been done by Switzerland. See Appendix XII.
For a discussion of the relation between democratic liberties
and totalitarian movements, cf. Emery Reves, *A Democratic
Manifesto*, Random House, New York, 1942, Chapter III.

the world of the future to the cause of democratic freedom. We may hope and we may believe they will not
refuse. The proof that they have accepted they alone can
give — in the measures they take when the war is over to
validate their own constitutional promises, and to make
free, equal, and reciprocal the exchange of news and
opinion between their own people and their present
allies.

If they refuse, we can still do our very best to get on
with them, persisting through the ordinary channels of
diplomacy in the effort to prevent a third World War.
But if they refuse, it will be better not to deceive ourselves, and to become relaxed in the semblance, which
will have little reality, of a universal society for the
maintenance of peace.

7. *Why Raise the Issue?*

The reader may be asking why raise this issue, and
seek an affirmative solution, when we already have re-
peated and unequivocal pledges by the Soviet government that its foreign policy supports democracy and not
totalitarianism? Does not the whole discussion impugn
the sincerity of the Soviet government, and emphasize
distrust of its intentions at the very moment when we
are allies at the climax of a great war and are determined,
if we can, to remain their "friends, in fact, in spirit, and
in purpose"? [7]

Though at first it may not seem so, it is in Russia's

[7] Declaration at Teheran, December 1, 1943. Appendix
IX.

vital interest and our own that the profound issue which divides us be brought into the full light of day and settled boldly and conclusively. Between Russia and the Western World there is a distrust which is ancient and deep. It is at least as old as the great schism of the Dark Ages which divided Christendom between Rome and Byzantium. The distrust has persisted into the modern era — under kings and czars, in democracies and soviets. It will not disappear suddenly or easily. By one means alone can the distrust be in the end dissolved, and that is by the acceptance and avowal of the same ultimate standards of value.

Only the inviolability of the human spirit can ever be the criterion of a universal standard. Nothing else unites all men beneath their differences. The outward and visible sign of faith in this inviolability is, in the realm of politics, to guarantee freedom of thought and expression, and thus to found government upon the continuing consent of the governed. When these guaranties are effective, a national state is affirming its adherence to the only conceivable standard of morals which can be universal. And without a universal standard of morals, a universal society does not exist.

It does not impugn the sincerity of the Soviet government to say that it cannot play its full part in a world society until it makes its own constitutional guaranties operative. It is not only possible, but indeed most probable, that the constitutional guaranties of 1936 have been in abeyance because after 1936, when Hitler had remilitarized the Rhineland, it was manifest that this gigantic war was coming. Desperate wars cannot be fought efficiently with democratic freedom; and Russia, where democratic freedom is a radical innovation, could hardly have risked the confusion when she was about to be ferociously attacked. But with the complete defeat of Germany and Japan, which are Russia's only enemies, the reasons for maintaining the dictatorship and martial law will be gone. If, nevertheless, they were maintained, how could it be explained?

The Russians simply cannot expect the rest of the world to believe in the democratic principles of their new foreign policy if they do not then practise those principles at home. And if the world distrusts Russian foreign policy, there is no way in which the Russians can make their policy work. Nothing could be more fatal to the Russian policy than to let the fear of bolshevism engender anti-Russian policy and fascism in the rest of the world.

It is vital to Russia herself that this fear be dissolved. Actually it would serve the Russian interest not only to repudiate, as she has already done, international communism, but to look without disfavor upon the legal outlawry and suppression by democratic states of all revolutionary parties. Russia would be infinitely more secure in the world if all the Western democracies followed the Swiss example. Russia would be freer to pursue her immense social projects if there were no communist parties and factions in the Atlantic Community providing fuel for the fires of fascist hostility to Russia. Switzerland, which has remained an island of true democracy in a sea of fascism, has shown that resistance to fascism is fortified by suppressing revolutionary communism.

For democracy is nothing if it is not a positive faith and a way of life. It has the right and the duty, and it must have the energetic will, to defend itself against all its enemies.

8. *The American Purpose*

The history of our foreign relations has shown, I believe, that the great lasting commitments of the United States in the outer world are confirmed, in the last analysis, not by treaties and declarations but by the fact that they enlist the American democracy as the champion of democracy. When this democratic impulse becomes separated from the strategic and economic realities of the world, it leads us to quixotic and sentimental interventions, to disappointment, frustration, and cynicism, and into grave trouble. But this is the dynamic purpose which drives the American nation on, which drove it into the great commitment of the Monroe Doctrine and made it the champion of the independence and integrity of China.

It expresses in its intent, however much we may fail to be practical and prudent in our acts, the highest interest of the United States, which is to live in a world environment which contains no dangerous and alien powers.

PART FIVE

On the Formation of a Universal Society

CHAPTER XII

WAR AIMS: THEN AND NOW

I WOULD contend that the war aims which I am about to sum up are definite. They say what should be the relations of the United States with its allies and its present enemies.

This is the definite question that the makers of policy have to decide. This is what the people have to make up their minds about. The rest is negotiation, legislation, and administration. Only if the fundamental relationships are determined correctly can the Administration and the Congress have clear objectives for drafting, negotiating, and legislating the agreements and treaties, terms of armistice and of settlement, laws and appropriations covering our military policy and our international relations in the post-war era.

In summary form our war aims are that the United States: —

1. Should consolidate the strategic and diplomatic connections, already existing, of the Atlantic Community: that is to say with the British Commonwealth and Empire, with Pan-America, with France and her empire, with Belgium, the Netherlands, and their colonies, with Luxembourg, Nor-

way, Denmark, Iceland; and should strive to extend them to Portugal, Spain, Italy, Greece, Eire, and Sweden.

2. Should recognize as valid and proper the strategic system of the Russian Orbit, as including within it the states east of Germany and west of the Soviet Union. It should then, for the reasons given in the preceding chapter, make known to the Soviet government its view that collaboration in a general world organization will be true and free, or restricted and dubious, depending upon how far the member states — particularly the most powerful ones — maintain at home the democratic liberties which they wish to see advanced abroad.

3. Should recognize that China will be the center of a third strategic system destined to include the whole mainland of Eastern Asia bounded by the frontiers of the Soviet Union and of India, and that the end of the war with Japan will inaugurate a new epoch in Chinese-American relations. Though we must be deeply concerned with the maintenance of peace in Asia, we can no longer be, as we have been from the time of John Hay, specially committed to China. For while we could be the special champions of China when the center of China's activity was still along her coasts, in the interior of Asia we can have no such commitment. For it is beyond our reach.

4. Should recognize that in time the Moslem and the Hindu nations of North Africa, the Middle East, and Southern Asia will form regional systems of their own.

5. Should make it the primary aim of the Far East settlement that Japan shall not hold the balance of power in the Far East among China, the Soviet Union, and the United States; should make it the primary aim of the German settlement that Germany shall not hold the balance of power between the Atlantic Community and the Russian Orbit.

6. Should recognize that the general aim of any lasting settlement of a war of aggression is to extinguish the war party and to protect the peace party, by making the defeat irrevocable and the peace acceptable.

It is my conviction that by following these lines of policy, the nations can come to rest in a long peace. Here is an order of power in which the vital interests of all the states capable of waging a great war are secured and are in equilibrium. It is not a mere diplomatic mechanism based on legal fictions, and then superimposed upon the real action of national states. It is a definite order of power among the national states of the world today: it is definite because it requires them to fix and stabilize their foreign policy with their neighbors. They do not surrender their sovereignty; they do reform their unpredictability and their vacillation, and they do forgo their right of arbitrary diplomatic maneuver in international relations. And I hold that only upon the stable foundations of such an ordered peace can a successful universal society be established.

1. The Error of 1919

This has not been, I realize, the prevailing American view since the days of President Wilson. He believed that a universal society like the League of Nations could be charged with the making and the keeping of peace. In this inquiry I take the radically different view, that held at the close, though not at the beginning, of the First World War by Theodore Roosevelt in this country, and by Georges Clemenceau abroad. It is that the deeper issues which are likely to disturb the peace must be settled not by the universal society, but in order that the universal society may have a chance to live and prosper. I do not believe that the security of the vital interests of the United States can be, should be, or will be entrusted to the collective security which a new and tentative international institution can be counted on to provide.

For ourselves, in the world as it is, we are certain to rely first upon our own armed power and national strength, then upon our natural allies, and then upon a general world organization. We shall not look upon the general organization as a substitute for our own measures of security but as a means of reinforcing them. If that is so, we must not expect Great Britain, the Soviet Union, China, France, or any other country to place a greater reliance upon collective security than we ourselves do. We shall wish to enter the universal society, having first made ourselves as secure as we can. They will do likewise.

It is now agreed among the governments that the general world organization, which the four great powers have promised to establish,[1] is not to be charged with settling this war. That, as the Moscow Agreement states, is the task of the four principal Allies consulting with members of the United Nations. But it is widely supposed, and perhaps even implied in the Agreement, that the general organization will in the near future become the guardian of the peace of the world. I am contending that we cannot rely upon it to do that. To prevent another war of aggression by our present enemies, we must rely upon the terms of peace — and upon pacts which bind together the Allies to enforce the terms of peace. Even less should we conceive the general world organization as being charged with preventing some other great theoretical war in which, let us say, the Soviet Union, China, Britain, and America are enemies. Quite the contrary, I think: a war among the founders of the universal society must be prevented in order that the society may survive. It cannot be prevented by the rules and procedures of the universal society but only by the direct recognition of national interests and their mutual accommodation. The world organization cannot police the policemen. If that is what it is supposed to do, it will not only fail, as did the League, but it will almost certainly excite tensions and alignments which will hasten its failure.

This was, in essence, the French view in 1919, and we

[1] See: Joint Four-Nation Agreement signed at Moscow October 30, 1943. Appendix VII.

must now admit, I believe, that Clemenceau was right and that Wilson was wrong. In 1919 what the world needed first of all was a lasting settlement with Germany: convincing measures for keeping Germany at peace until her ruling classes, who had made the war, died out and the Germans of the Weimar Republic were firmly in power and had acquired the habits of democratic government. Wilson's insistence on making the German settlement secondary to a plan of universal and perpetual peace denied France the security which only dependable allies could have provided; the weakness of the French inhibited a magnanimous treatment of the Weimar Republic. For since the German settlement would not be enforced, the Weimar Republic was at the mercy of the war party, which had gone underground and was conspiring against it.

By preferring peace in general to a specific peace, President Wilson in effect forgot about Germany. He assumed that the armistice had settled the German question. He then went to Paris to impose a Wilsonian peace on the Allies.[2] Despite the warnings of men like Theodore Roosevelt, Lodge, Knox, and others,[3] President Wilson dissolved the coalition which had won the war and

[2] Cf. Stephen Bonsal, *Unfinished Business*, Doubleday Doran & Company, Inc., New York, 1944, p. 2.

[3] On November 27, 1918, Theodore Roosevelt issued a statement which said: "It is our business to act with our allies and to show an undivided front with them against any move of our late enemies. . . . In the present war we have won only by standing shoulder to shoulder with our

could alone have perpetuated the settlement. He engendered a useless and pernicious quarrel with Italy over the insignificant port of Fiume; in this quarrel Italian fascism, through the exploits of d'Annunzio, got its start. In fact, the attention of the Allies became so diverted from Germany [4] that the Peace Conference found itself

---

allies and presenting an undivided front to the enemy. It is our business to show the same loyalty and good faith at the Peace Conference. . . . Let every difference of opinion be settled among the Allies themselves, and then let them impose their common will on the nations responsible for the hideous disaster which has almost wrecked mankind."

Senator Lodge, speaking in the Senate December 21, 1918, said: "The attempt to form now a league of nations — and I mean an effective league, with power to enforce its decrees — no other is worth discussing — can tend at this moment only to embarrass the peace which we ought to make at once with Germany. . . . Is not the first duty of all the countries united against Germany to make a peace with Germany? Is that not the way to bring peace to the world now? . . . To attempt in any way to separate us from our allies now, or to prevent perfect unity of action, is as harmful as such efforts were when we were fighting in Northern France and on the plains of Flanders."

And Senator Knox on December 18, 1918, had asked: Could we "create a League with purer conscience or higher ideals than the one called into existence by the German attack? Wise policy, as opposed to shallow empiricism, would seem to counsel us to solidify and build upon what we have tried, rather than plunge headlong into a universal experiment."

[4] On August 11, 1920, Viscount d'Abernon, the British Ambassador to Germany after the war, at this time a mem-

waging several little military campaigns in Russia.[5] The Allies also entangled themselves in pledges of disarmament which led the British to worry because France was too well-armed (!), and prompted us to launch a crusade which disarmed the British and ourselves.

We must not repeat the error of counting upon a world organization to establish peace. The responsibility for order rests upon the victorious governments. They cannot delegate this responsibility to a world society which does not yet exist or has just barely been organized. We must establish peace specifically and directly in the world as we shall find it — by maintaining the combined defenses of the Atlantic nations, by continuing the great coalition with the Soviet Union and with China, by making it impossible for Germany and Japan to undo the settlement of this war and to separate the victors.

The organized power which wins the war must be used to win the peace. It can bring to an end the frightful wars of our age. If it cannot, then nothing can, cer-

---

ber of the Anglo-French mission in Poland, wrote in his diary: "I have just written to Hankey on the importance of obtaining German co-operation against the Soviet. News from Paris is to the effect that the German diplomatic representatives there are constantly fishing for an invitation from the Entente to use German military force against the Soviet. . . . If a good bargain could be made with the Germans I should vote for it."

[5] Cf. George Stewart, *The White Armies of Russia*, The Macmillan Company, New York, 1933; Foster Rhea Dulles, *The Road to Teheran*, Princeton University Press, Princeton, N. J., 1944.

tainly not some pale, thin, abstract, generalized blueprint of a mechanism.

2. *The Work of a Universal Society*

The true function of the universal society is to facilitate intercourse among nations already at peace. This task — of maintaining standards and instituting reforms, which were nonpolitical and more concerned with individual than with national security — the League of Nations performed exceedingly well.[6] It would have done it better and better if only the world had remained at peace, and when peace comes again, the work will be resumed and expanded.

If the new world society is not burdened with the task of preventing great wars among the great powers, it can do much to prevent, regulate, and compose the disputes that are not directly and closely related to the greatest issues of war and peace. We know that hard cases do not make good law; it is in the treatment of the easier cases that principles of international comity will develop, and decisions will be rendered that become precedents, expanding the common law of the nations.

Again, provided it is not burdened with the vital relations of the great powers, the world society may accomplish much to relieve and transmute the problems of empire. In Africa and elsewhere there are many peoples who are too primitive for independence. Prin-

[6] Cf. Arthur Sweetser, "The Non-Political Achievements of the League," *Foreign Affairs*, October 1940.

ciples and standards of trusteeship will have to be developed. In the Middle East and Southern Asia there are gifted and ancient nations which, nevertheless, are just reaching, but have not attained, modern statehood; how they are to enter into the world society is as yet obscure and is fraught with grave and even explosive difficulties. The older and more solidly established states, the founding members of the world society, cannot afford to have divergent policies and competing standards of conduct in their relations with these peoples. Above all we must continue the experience of co-operation in practical affairs so well illustrated in the combined boards. The world society can provide additional organs of information, study and agreement, and a favorable moral climate.

Not only in these regions but everywhere, the world society can do much to facilitate the exchange of scientific knowledge, inventions, technology, and of cultural achievements. Close intercourse among diverse peoples does not always make them friends: it is most surely beneficent among men and women who devote their lives to the arts and sciences. For though they have all the ordinary human characteristics, they have passed through a professional discipline, and they are not primarily concerned with the issues of profit and power in the struggle for existence.

The principles of these constructive works cannot all be defined in advance and laid down by fiat and pronunciamento. They will have to be imagined and invented. They will have to be put together by precedents, developed out of practical experience in combating disease, destitution, and ignorance; in working out projects for the conservation and development of the natural resources of the earth, the improvement of transportation and communication; in arranging for an orderly extension of international commerce.

We shall be wise, I believe, to dismiss from our minds the idea that the universal society is the embryo of a world government charged with policing mankind in order to prevent war. We should conceive it as a society devoted to cultivating the arts of peace, leaving to the direct and specific diplomatic relations of the national states, acting within regional groups such as I have described, the problems of their security and the prevention of war.

If the world organization is charged with the tremendous issues of war or peace, it will, I believe, become a forum in which differences are accentuated by public debate, and agreements obstructed because they call for public compromises which appear humiliating. We shall not, I believe, further the comity of nations by establishing an international assembly of which the avowed purpose is that every nation is there to inspect and police every other nation.

Let us not be so naïve as to think that the great issues of war and peace, upon which hangs the life of nations, will or can be settled by public debates and public voting in an international assembly. Matters of life and death cannot be submitted to a conglomerate parliament of mankind. The critical decisions must in any event be threshed out first in quiet and in confidence by those who have the responsibility because they have the power. To envelop the tremendous business of keeping the peace in the gossip and intrigues of the lobbies and corridors of an international assembly will not make more likely the triumph of justice and reason. On the contrary, every time the assembly is scheduled to meet, the tension in world affairs will rise. The propagandists will be at work in advance, and the meetings will tend to take place in an atmosphere of crisis and climax. We shall get drama when we want accommodation and compromise.

It will be much better if the meetings of the assembly are concerned with unexciting, with more or less technical, projects for doing something that is positively and undeniably useful and good. For while war can be prevented only by the proper organization of power, international collaboration can become a habit by the practice of collaboration. There must then be many concrete things to collaborate about. These concrete things cannot be the things men ordinarily fight about: their frontiers, their sovereignty, their security. They must be the things they do not ordinarily fight about. These are the arts of peace.

The decision not to charge the world society with the task of preventing war by policing the world will, I believe, make it more likely that war will be prevented. For it will fix the responsibility where alone it can be discharged — upon the governments of the great powers and their neighbors with whom they are allied. There will be no pretense, and no escape by means of the pretense, that the responsibility for preventing war is anywhere else than where it really is: in the great military states themselves.

CHAPTER XIII

THE WILSONIAN PRINCIPLES

THE JUDGMENTS of men of good will are still shaped in the molds of Woodrow Wilson's thought. His name is now so completely identified with the ideal of a universal society that the principles he laid down for attaining a universal society are generally believed to be axiomatic and immutable.[1] Field Marshal Smuts has said "not Wilson, but humanity, failed at Paris." The seventeen points of Secretary Hull's foreign policy,[2] the eight points of the Atlantic Charter,[3] are in style and substance the Wilsonian code of international conduct. Once again, it is about to be said that not the code and the doctrine, but mankind, is failing.

Yet it is, I think, demonstrable that the ideal of a universal society cannot be realized by following the Wilsonian principles. His principles spring from the love of liberty and of justice, and are inspired by a righteous

[1] Few histories written since 1919 give an adequate account of the argument of President Wilson's opponents — not that of the irreconcilable isolationists, but that of men like Theodore Roosevelt, Root, Knox, and even Lodge, in this country. See footnote 3, pp. 162–163.

[2] March 21, 1944. Appendix XI.

[3] Appendix V.

compassion. But they do not and cannot produce liberty and justice and charity because in reality they disorganize the unity of states and their security. They do not make for an organized life but for disorder. In the disorder there can be only a brutal struggle for survival.

1. The Wilsonian Negatives

The Wilsonian general principles of international life were laid down in the six of the Fourteen Points which deal with general principles,[4] the Four Principles, the Four Ends, and the Five Particulars.[5]

When we examine these nineteen general principles, we find that they *are a series of prohibitions. They forbid national states to do the things which they have always done to defend their interests and to preserve their integrity.*

Point IV called for the reduction of national armaments "to the lowest point consistent with domestic safety." In the official commentary,[6] approved by President Wilson, domestic safety is interpreted as meaning "not only internal policing but the protection of territory against invasion." Thus Point IV is a prohibition against armaments sufficient to defend a region — the Caribbean, for example. If it observes this principle, a

[4] Points I–V and Point XIV.

[5] For texts, see Appendices I–IV.

[6] For the full text of the official commentary on the Fourteen Points cf. Charles Seymour, *The Intimate Papers of Colonel House*, Houghton Mifflin Company, Boston, 1928. Vol. IV, p. 192.

nation is limited to waiting passively on the defensive against actual invasion. For it may not be strong enough to forestall and prevent aggression which is being prepared against it: it may only try to repel the aggressor wherever and whenever he strikes. In the interval between the two wars British, French, and American military policy followed this disastrous prescription.

In the Four Ends of July 4, 1918, Wilson laid down the rule that "the settlement of *every* question, whether of territory, of sovereignty, of economic arrangement, or of political relationship" must be "upon the basis of the *free acceptance* of that settlement *by the people immediately concerned.*" This principle gives to the people inhabiting any strategic point upon the world's surface — say Panama, Gibraltar — an absolute veto on any arrangement designed to use that point for the security of a nation, a region, or of the world.

In the Five Particulars of September 27, 1918, Wilson stipulated that "there can be no leagues, or alliances or special covenants and understandings within the general and common family of the League of Nations." This prohibits nations which belong to one strategic area — the North American nations, the American republics, the Western European nations — from organizing a combined defense and from concerting their foreign policy.

Finally, Wilson identified himself with the principle of self-determination. Forgetting Abraham Lincoln, forgetting the greatest constitutional issue in the history of the United States, he never paused to define the difference between the right of self-determination and the right of secession. As a matter of fact, Wilson adopted the principle of self-determination as an expedient of war in order to promote rebellion in Austria-Hungary. As late as January, 1918, when he announced the Fourteen Points, he had not invoked it and I think he did not believe in it.

It was not necessary to invoke this exceedingly tricky general principle in order to justify the reconstitution of Poland, the independence of Czechoslovakia, and the creation of Yugoslavia. It would have been quite sufficient to give specific support to the Poles, the Czechoslovaks, and the Yugoslavs. To invoke the general principle of self-determination, and to make it a supreme law of international life, was to invite sheer anarchy.

For the principle can be and has been used to promote the dismemberment of practically every organized state. None knew this better than Adolf Hitler himself: the principle of self-determination was his chief instrument for enlarging the Reich by annexation, and for destroying from within the civil unity of the states he intended to attack. Hitler invoked this principle when he annexed Austria, dismembered Czechoslovakia, attacked Poland, undermined the unity of the Flemings and Walloons in Belgium, infiltrated Alsace-Lorraine, conspired against Russia in the Ukraine and in the Caucasus, tampered with Brazil, suborned the Arabs.

Thus at its worst the principle of self-determination is a license to intervention and aggression. In any event it is a counsel of despair. Despite its superficial "democracy" the principle of self-determination is in an exact sense deeply un-American and uncivilizing. For it rejects the civilized ideal, which is the American ideal, that comes down to us from the Roman world and has persisted in the great tradition of the West. It is the ideal of a state within which diverse peoples find justice and liberty under equal laws and become a commonwealth. Self-determination, which has nothing to do with self-government but has become confused with it, is barbarous and reactionary: by sanctioning secession, it invites majorities and minorities to be intransigent and irreconcilable. It is stipulated in the principle of self-determination that they need not be compatriots because they will soon be aliens. There is no end to this atomization of human society. Within the minorities who have seceded there will tend to appear other minorities who in their turn will wish to secede.

The Wilsonian principles disarm every state which must be counted on to enforce the peace. Armaments designed only to repel invasion from behind Maginot Lines cannot be used to enforce peace. The principles deny to every great state which is to be a founder and participant in a world order the right to meet its strategic needs. They forbid nations to combine the defenses of the strategic zone in which they live. They forbid them to concert the foreign policies of their neighborhoods so that there shall be no diverse entanglements for which the whole neighborhood must bear the consequences.

In short the Wilsonian principles prohibit the nations which are supposed to organize the world for peace from using any of the essential instruments of national and international action.

2. *A Double Standard of Morals*

The Wilsonian principles are prejudices formed in the Age of Innocence, in the century of American isolation. Wilson wished America to take its place in a universal society. But he was willing to participate only if the whole world acted as the United States had acted when it enjoyed isolation during the nineteenth century. The United States had then had no need to arm, no need to find alliances, no need to take strategic precautions; Wilson's principles were a demand that the whole world take vows to live forever after on the same terms. He supposed that international relations could then be conducted verbally by meetings at Geneva.

Military power, strategic positions and connections, alliances, the unity of historic states and their spheres of vital interest — all these instruments of international life — have, no doubt, been used frequently for aggression and domination. And that is why the Wilsonian gospel seemed at first to be the promise of salvation itself. But the gospel did not bring salvation. It was followed by, and it had a large part in bringing on, the terrible paralysis of the democratic nations. Between 1919 and 1940 they were brought to the verge of a total catastrophe; they acted almost as if they had lost the will to live. The free nations were indoctrinated with the principles of disarmament, of the passive defensive, of isolation from their allies, and of secession, called self-determination. The disarmed, isolated, and disunified democracies were thrown into utter moral confusion when these negative principles, which had been proclaimed the only moral principles, were invoked against them in the Rhineland, in Austria, at Munich, and in the negotiations over Russian support of Poland.

The great Wilsonian misconception lies in the supposition that a universal society, a League such as was founded at Geneva in 1919, "a general international organization" such as has again been promised at Moscow in 1943, can *replace* the ordinary instruments of international life. This misconception persists in high and influential quarters and among the general public. It threatens to render abortive the organization of a world order. For while a universal society can reinsure national and regional security, it is not a substitute for solid frontiers, adequate and rationally planned armed force, strategic position, alliances among natural and necessary allies. For these reasons we shall not disarm ourselves and emasculate our own foreign policy and then put our whole trust in an international organization. We must not ask, we must not expect, we must not wish, others to do what we shall not do.

A double standard of morals in our foreign policy will not make for the sanctity of moral principles in international life. For though the Wilsonian principles are nothing if not moral in purpose, and can scarcely be criticized without an appearance of challenging the eternal verities, they are nevertheless contrary to the Golden Rule. They hold others to a standard which we do not ourselves observe.

Thus the United States does not mean, and never has meant, to reduce its national armaments to a point where they sufficed merely to protect the "domestic" territory of the forty-eight states against invasion. We have never thought of renouncing the defense of the Panama Canal, or of our naval base in the independent republic of Cuba, or the defense of Canada, Mexico, and the Caribbean nations. We have never thought of acknowledging the "right" of Cuba or Haiti or the Republic of Panama — all of them independent sovereign states — to contract alliances which were inconsistent with the concert of the whole North American region. And as we fought a great civil war for union and against the right of secession, the general principle of self-determination is certainly not a part of our philosophy.

To preach a moral code which its authors do not accept is to promote disrespect for the moral law.[7]

3. *The Unavowed Wilsonian Principles*

It has seemed to me necessary to examine the Wilsonian doctrine because it continues to be the official doc-

[7] Cf. Bonsal, *op. cit.*, on Wilson's asking for a reservation on the Monroe Doctrine (Article 21 of the Covenant).

trine. What is said still conforms with it. But what is done by the United States and by its allies does not conform with the doctrine. Because it is impossible to make practice fit the theory, the nation remains divided, is morally confused, wonders whether it is for America first or something else first, and is afflicted with a sense of guilt. I hold that the theory is wrong, and that the practice cannot be made right until the theory is revised. The Wilsonian principles lead us up a blind ally. They are not the true alternative to isolation, and as long as they shape American thinking our efforts to make an ordered peace will fail.

We must ask ourselves how President Wilson and his disciples could believe that these negative principles would promote a universal society. I think it was because they were assuming that they were laying the foundations of a world state under a world government. The Wilsonian principles, which are irrational in the world we live in, are quite rational if we imagine that the nations are about to do what the thirteen American states did when they formed the Federal Union. The Constitution says to our states just what the Wilsonian principles say to the nations of the world, that "no state shall enter into any treaty, alliance, or confederation" . . . that "no state shall, without the consent of Congress . . . keep troops or ships of war in time of peace, or enter into any agreement or compact with another state." [8] President Wilson proposed to disarm the nations just as the

[8] Article I, Section 10.

federal government has disarmed the states. Assume that we are establishing a federal government of the world, a superstate sovereign above all existing national states, and the Wilsonian negatives are logical.

That Wilson himself realized the implications of his doctrine is reasonably clear. When he was confronted with Senator Hitchcock's opinion that many Senators would ask for reservations on the Monroe Doctrine and the right to withdraw from the League, Wilson explained them to his colleagues in Paris,[9] saying: "One of my difficulties is that Americans demand complete assurance that they are not being called upon to give up the sovereignty of their states. I am confident, however, that the day is near when they will become as eager partisans of the sovereignty of mankind as they are now of their national or state sovereignty. But, for the moment, it is necessary to take into consideration current prejudices and make concessions to their sense of independence, of will and action. I confess I would find myself in a very awkward position if the amendment is not approved."

This casts a vivid light upon the cause of the moral and intellectual confusion which has paralyzed this country for twenty-five years. To Wilson, the apostle of the new international order, the real object was the surrender of national sovereignty to the sovereignty of mankind. But because of what he regarded as current prejudices, he had to make concessions which concealed and denied the real object.

[9] Bonsal, *op. cit.*, p. 159.

When Wilson found that he could not create a world state under the sovereignty of mankind, he did not realize that he could no longer hold to his principles of military and diplomatic disarmament and of self-determination.

Since 1919 the position of the Wilsonians has been like that which Hamilton and Madison would have been in if the federal Constitution had not been ratified. But if no federal government had been established, would New York and Virginia, for example, have been told by Hamilton and Madison that as sovereign states they must not do the things which the federal Constitution forbids them to do? That is what the Wilsonians continue to tell the nations.

4. The Moral Order

It is indubitably true, as Wilson had the vision to see, that the international society must rest at last upon the acceptance of common principles of conduct. But they must be principles which men can believe in and can live by. The Wilsonian principles did not and cannot meet this test. They are negative rules which, though meant to prohibit aggression and tyranny, in fact prohibit national states from making the provisions which will insure their own survival against aggression and tyranny. To end the struggle for power Wilson sought to make the nations powerless. The Wilsonian principles stipulate that the nations should disarm themselves physically and politically and then entrust their independence and their vital interests to an assembly of debating diplomats. This is like arguing that because the Bible says the love of money is the root of all evil, none should work for money and all should depend on the charity of their neighbors.

The cynicism which corroded the democracies in the interval between the two German wars was engendered by a moral order which was in fact a moral frustration. Field Marshal Smuts overlooked this when he pronounced the judgment that not Wilson but humanity failed at Paris. The moralists at Paris gave humanity a code of morality which no one could observe, which, in so far as its prohibitions had influence in disarming the nations, disaggregating alliances, and disrupting great states, was a preparation not for peace under the law but for aggression in the midst of anarchy. The moral code failed because it was not a good moral code.

We too shall fail to find a moral basis for the international order if we do not discern and then correct the spiritual error which underlies the Wilsonian misconception. It is the error of forgetting that we are men and of thinking that we are gods. We are not gods. We do not have the omniscience to discover a new moral law and the omnipotence to impose it upon mankind. When we draw up lists of general principles which we say are universal, to which we mean to hold everyone, we are indulging in a fantasy. We are imagining ourselves as beings who are above and outside mankind, detached from the concrete realities of life itself, and able to govern the world by fiat. But in fact we are inside the human world. We are mere mortals with limited power and little universal wisdom.

We shall collaborate best with other nations if we start with the homely fact that their families and their homes, their villages and lands, their countries and their own ways, their altars, their flags, and their hearths — not charters, covenants, blueprints, and generalities — are what men live for and will, if it is necessary, die for.

A sound moral code of international life will not prohibit men from relying at last upon their own virtue in defending and preserving the things they cherish more than life itself. It must not ask them to hazard their vital interests on schemes which, if they failed, would ruin them. A sound moral code must be rooted deeply in the things men live and die for. It must be the means of conserving these real things, and it must be so cogently, so candidly, so sincerely devoted to these deeply human and substantial ends that the code itself evokes their instinctive assent and their natural loyalty.

No code of international conduct can do this, I believe, which does not derive from the view that the world order can eventually be formed only by organizing from the national state, ascending through the regional neighborhood, and then to the larger communities and to a concert of great communities.

CHAPTER XIV

THE ASSOCIATION OF GREAT COMMUNITIES

A UNIVERSAL society can be only a voluntary association of sovereign states. It cannot be a world government because there is no way, now conceivable, by which this government could obtain from the 1500 million inhabitants of the earth the power to legislate and to execute its laws. There can, of course, be no hereditary right of rulership in a world government, and there is no way of electing a world government. No one can think of a rational rule by which all the adults who are citizens of all the member states could be organized into constituencies for the election of world officials. The people of the United States, who have so great a responsibility for world order, would not, for example, concede sovereign powers to a world legislature in which, on the basis of one vote one man, they were outvoted ten to one by the inhabitants of Asia. And, yet, on what moral principle could Americans claim that their votes should count more heavily than those of other human beings?

An institution is not a government unless at the very minimum it can make some laws that it can enforce upon individuals; unless at least it can levy some taxes and collect them, conscript armies and equip them. But if the world institution cannot be elected by the people, then it can exercise only such powers as are delegated and contributed by the existing governments.

Were all the existing governments autocracies, it is conceivable that they could be leagued together, as feudal princes were united, to constitute a world empire. Some have feared that this would be the outcome of the nuclear alliance of the four great powers. They need not fear it: certainly in the Atlantic Community no government can long exercise power without the consent of the people. The only possible world society is a voluntary association of national states. These states might, if they thought it advisable, agree by treaty to contribute funds and their military quotas to a world institution. This would not be a government. For the contributions would depend not upon the will of the world authority but upon the willingness of the national governments to continue making their contributions. As long as the world institution cannot be elected by the people of the world, it can have no power except that which is contributed and delegated voluntarily by the sovereign national states.

Now if the world officials have to get their actual power from the existing governments, then, no matter what the covenants and charters may say, the world organization is a voluntary association of diplomats who confer. If so, let us not wrap it up in different words.

If that is what it is, it will be a better association of diplomats by treating it as such, and acting accordingly.

1. A World Council

We can set up a world council. It will not be a world government in which world governors rule mankind: it will be a council where governments consult. They can only consult and negotiate and try to agree. For questions which national states regard as vital cannot be decided by putting them to a vote.

In 1937 there were seventy-three states with a recognizable claim to separate representation in a world organization.[1] It is evident that if all qualified members had a vote and if all had to agree, no serious controversy could be decided by counting votes. Even if the parties to a serious dispute were not allowed to vote, it is in the highest degree unlikely that they could not find some backers and friends among the voting states. The whole conception of voting in the universal society is, it seems to me, based on a misapprehension.

The question of admitting new members compounds

[1] The most inclusive international organization existing before the war was the Postal Union. It had seventy-two members; only Nepal was not a member. Sixty-three were at one time or another signatories of the Covenant, the absentees being Lichtenstein, Monaco, Nepal, San Marino, Danzig, Iceland, Saudi Arabia, the United States, Vatican City, and Yemen.

In 1937, of the recognized sovereign states sixty-six had more than 500,000 inhabitants.

the difficulty. Nothing is more likely than that in the near future many subject peoples will demand their independence and ask for recognition by the universal society of states. If each member has a vote and a veto, the balance of voting power will be altered by admitting a new member. We have only to remember the outcry in this country because Britain had "six votes" in the League to our "one," or the shudder of apprehension when the Soviet Union announced that it was now composed of sixteen republics with sixteen foreign offices. Many, who think international affairs can be governed by political mechanics, began to ask whether the United States ought not to claim forty-eight votes! The notion of conducting a universal society by counting votes leads to such absurdities.

Movements of national independence would be judged by the older members as the Northern and Southern states of the Union judged the admission of slave or free states in the era before our Civil War. They would promote independence where they felt sure the new state would vote with them. They would oppose independence in a nation that might vote against them. Should the United States make Puerto Rico an independent state and gain one more vote in the world council; or should Russia foster an independent Puerto Rico in the hope of gaining from their grateful protégé a vote to offset that of the United States?

This is the *reductio ad absurdum* of the whole conception of a world order in which decisions are made by the votes of all the recognized governments, always increasing in number under the Wilsonian principle of self-determination.

2. Regionalism and Peace

If our analysis is in general correct, then the shape of things to come is going to be unlike the design of the League of Nations as it was set up in Geneva or as the champions of collective security have, during this war, usually envisaged it. The ultimate ideal of a world at peace under the reign of law is not at issue. But the manner in which the peoples of the world can and will and should organize themselves is very much at issue.

The question is whether some sixty to seventy states, each acting separately, can form a universal organization for the maintenance of peace. I contend that they cannot, and that single sovereign states must combine in their neighborhoods, and that the neighborhoods must combine into larger communities and constellations, which then participate in a universal society.

Between these opposing conceptions the issue is profound and momentous. Objections present themselves at once to the views expounded in this book: they are that the world will be divided up into spheres of influence each dominated by a great power, that within these spheres the smaller and the weaker states will come under the influence of the great power, and that the huge constellations of states may become rivals and enemies. We cannot minimize the force of these objections, and I do not. Yet these regional groupings already exist, particularly in our own region, and they are forming elsewhere, and I do not believe that we can organize the world by ignoring or condemning and outlawing them. On the contrary, I believe that only by perfecting these regional groupings can we hope to make any progress towards stabilizing international relations.

Let me illustrate. Assume, as the Wilsonians do, that the foreign relations of each state are the equal concern of every state. Let us ask ourselves, then, whether we believe that a dispute between the United States and the Republic of Panama should be settled "collectively" by an assembly of mankind? It is quickly evident that the United States will not wish it settled by the world council. Why not? The Republic of Panama is a sovereign state. According to the Wilsonian doctrine, its relations with the United States cannot be special, and different from its relations with China and Russia. Yet we should object to Russian or Chinese intervention in the dispute. On the other hand, we should almost certainly invite Mexico and Brazil to participate in settling the dispute. We should feel that they are entitled to participate because they belong to the same neighborhood, and its good order is their proper concern. But if Russia and China reached out to take a hand in the situation, or if Panama, turning its back on its neighbors, called upon Russia and China to take a hand, the dispute would at once become entangled with other disputes in other parts of the world. Britain and France would have to take a hand because Russia and China had taken a hand. The Panamanian question would then be in the same pot with, let us say, the Burmese, the Lebanese, the Persian, the Outer Mongolian questions. How China voted about Panama might then depend on how we voted on Burma.

Thus a dispute which ought to be settled within the region would be inflated into a global dispute.

We may grant that in a regional settlement might would tend to make right. But is there any reason to think that in a global settlement more perfect justice would be done? There is none whatever. The global settlement would not be pure justice. It would be the net result of the pressure and logrolling of all the great powers; it would be a deal in which the claims of Panama would have been thrown into the scales with those of Burma, Lebanon, Persia, Mongolia, and so forth. And worse still, there might be no settlement, not even a compromise and a deal. Panama would then remain an open sore, one among many, infected with the virus of global war.

If it is undesirable to make the Panamanian question a global question, then the constitution of the world society should not be based on the assumption that everything is everybody's business. We must not write into the constitution of the world society a license to universal intervention. For if we license it, we shall invite it. If we invite it, we shall get it. And when we get it, we shall resist it, none more obstinately than the people of the United States.

It will be said that there is no justice in the world if the small Republic of Panama cannot take its appeal against the United States to the society of nations. Of course, Panama can appeal. There is always an appeal to the conscience of mankind. That does not mean that every government should be invited to intervene everywhere, and that everybody's business should be everybody's business. I am contending that the intervention of governments outside the neighborhood should be regarded as a last resort only in exceptional cases.

Our own traditions and our practice commit us to this view. Americans discovered and have practised with considerable success the regionalism of the Monroe Doctrine, the Pan-American Union, and the Good Neighbor Policy; why should they now be the exponents in other parts of the world of a universalist doctrine, which is the very opposite?

The evil for which we have to find a remedy is the shifting alliances of "power politics." The remedy for shifting alliances is to stabilize alliances. Regionalism seeks to do just that; each state would recognize that it belongs to one, and only one, larger strategic zone of security. Its alignment would not be in doubt, would not be the subject of intrigue and bargaining. For the calculable future each state would be the member of a community of states, with which it must concert its military defenses and its foreign policy. It would be an unfriendly act if it seceded from its community and joined another, or entered into special relations outside its community unless with the full consent of its neighbors.

It will be feared that great constellations like the Atlantic Community, the Russian Orbit, and the Chinese Community will become engaged in a titanic conflict. The members of these communities are now engaged in a titanic conflict, and in order to survive they have had to organize, impromptu and tardily, the strategical combinations which, in my view, they ought to maintain and perfect. It cannot be said that this titanic conflict was caused by regional combinations. It can be said that it was not prevented and has very nearly been lost because they did not exist.

No one can be perfectly certain that the Atlantic Community and the Russian Orbit, if they are formed, will not quarrel and go to war. But one can say that to stabilize the alliances and military establishments of all states is to remove the most provoking forms of interference and intervention which, because they menace the vital security of great states, are a cause of great wars.

3. Conclusion

The argument developed in this book is that we should reverse the Wilsonian principles: that we should seek to conserve the existing political states, rather than to dismember them on the ground of self-determination, and that we should approve, not forbid, should perfect and not dissolve, the regional grouping of national states. The true constituents of the universal society would not then be seventy-three political molecules, likely to split up into no one knows how many atoms; the universal society would be the association of the great communities of mankind.

One of them, our own, I have called for want of a better name the Atlantic Community. It already exists, not because a theorist invented it, but because in the necessity of a war of survival we have had to organize it. The Atlantic Community now consists of great historic formations. They are the progeny of Western Christendom. They are Pan-America, the British Commonwealth of Nations, France and her Latin neighbors, the Low Countries, and Scandinavia.

When the series of German wars of aggression is definitively terminated, this Western community will come to include Germany and perhaps all of Europe to the borders of the Soviet Union. But the menace of another German war of aggression cannot be thoroughly disposed of in less than one generation — not until the war party has died out leaving no heirs. During this period the world must live under a special regime if it is to make certain that there is not to be a third World War in the next generation. For this period the Atlantic Community from the West, the states of Eastern Europe acting within the Russian Orbit, will have to organize their military establishments and co-ordinate their foreign policies for the express purpose of preventing Germany from recovering her military power by holding the balance of power between the Soviet Union and the Western World.

Our object then is not to disintegrate the historic communities but to conserve them and associate them more closely. We are at war in Asia, as well as in Europe, for this principle: we would not connive at the dismemberment of China and the destruction of its independence. For fifty years we have insisted, though China is not yet a well-organized state, that China is one of the true historic formations, and that it must not be shattered into atoms, that an equal place must be reserved for the great Chinese Community in the council of the world.

The historic communities of states are well worth preserving. If the historic communities are worth preserving, then they, not separate states and certainly not individual persons, are the constituent members of the universal society. The issues that are local within them they must settle among themselves; the issues that are general they will deal with in the world council, consulting at the higher level after they have consulted at the lower levels, deliberating not as disparate sovereign states but as communities which have in the end a common interest.

In this view of things the horrid antithesis between nationalism and internationalism subsides. No one is asked to transfer his allegiance from his own country to a new cosmopolitan fatherland. As he is a good patriot so he is a good neighbor, and by being a good neighbor he is loyal to the laws, the usages, and the requirements of the universal society.

There can be no conflict, I maintain, between a sound national and a wise international policy. It is the acid test of a sound policy that if it cannot be consummated completely it nevertheless need not fail utterly. The proposals of this book do, I think, meet this test. We can advance toward a universal society. But should we fail to arrive, we can stand with great advantage upon the order which the United States, Britain, the Soviet Union, and China can establish by maintaining the coalition they have formed in this war. If, however, we cannot hold this achievement, we can still find a large measure of security within the Atlantic Community. If this community falls apart, as it so nearly did in 1940, then our final stand is with our nearest neighbors in North America.

Our views will not be the right views until they reconcile the conflict of opinion by which this country has been rent and paralyzed for a quarter of a century. In this dispute the so-called isolationists were demonstrably blind to the strategic realities of American security; they did not see how or why the conquest of China by Japan, and of Western Europe by Germany, would threaten the Western Hemisphere and the very life of the United States itself. But on the whole their opponents have been equally blind: as the alternative to isolation they argued that the nation should rely upon collective security as a substitute for its own armed strength and the diplomatic protection of its vital interests. So they irritated and provoked the blind but deep national instinct of self-preservation.

We have to reverse the Wilsonian pattern of collective security. We cannot build a universal society from the top downwards. We must build up to it from the existing national states and historic communities. That, I think, is what we must learn from the great experiment at Geneva and from its failure. We have, I am convinced, to learn it thoroughly. For we cannot afford to fail again.

CHAPTER XV

AFTERWORD

THIS IS a little book on a big subject. It is a little book because it can only be one man's view, and it has a big subject because it is an effort to discern the position of the United States in the shape of things to come.

When I attempt to compare the America in which I was reared with the America of today, I am struck by how unconcerned I was as a young man with the hard questions which are the subject matter of history. I did not think about the security of the Republic and how to defend it. I did not think about intercourse with the rest of the world, and how to maintain it. I did not think about the internal order of the nation, and how the needs and the work of our people were to be kept in balance with the resources of the nation.

Yet these very things that I never thought about at the time have since proved to be paramount. Man's struggle for existence still breaks out into wars and revolutions. In my age of innocence I thought that the struggle for existence had long since been happily concluded. We know now that it has not been.

1. The Age of Innocence

The crucial difference, as I see it, between the recent American past and the American future is that we have come to the end of our effortless security and of our limitless opportunities. This portends a future very different from our past. We shall live much less privately. The personal life of the individual will be bound up with his public life as a citizen.

Until very recently, and for so long a time that no one living could remember anything else, the United States had no enemies. The nation enjoyed such perfect immunity from attack that it could dispense almost entirely with the trouble, the costs, and the risks of armaments, strategic precautions, and alliances. We explained this effortless security by a popular myth: the Atlantic Ocean was too wide for an enemy to cross it. What went on across the seas would never trouble us if we did not trouble it. The United States then did not need measures to provide for its own security; it needed merely to abstain from becoming involved across the seas. Only in the second of the two great wars of this century are our people recognizing the fact that the period of our unique, effortless security is ended, and that the United States has now to be *defended*, like all the other great states of history, by diplomacy, by policy, and by arms.

Moreover, from its colonial beginnings until the turn of this century, the country was on balance an importer of manufactures from Europe and a borrower of foreign capital. As such it could not have, and did not need to have, a foreign economic policy. The foreign creditor makes the policy to which the colonial borrower conforms. Until the First World War, when the United States itself became the leading creditor nation of the world, the responsibility for maintaining and regulating the terms of international trade was in London and the other European financial capitals. It was not in Washington or in New York. When Americans borrowed what they needed from Europe and sold what Europe was willing to buy, they did not have to have a foreign economic policy. They did not have to think about how they could balance their foreign accounts. The accounts were balanced by London finance, which operated and managed what Americans call the gold standard. No special effort and no public action were required here, and so it seemed as if the gold standard worked impersonally and automatically, without human guidance. This notion took its place in our mythology along with the notion that the oceans are so wide that they are impassable.

At home since the beginning of this century there have no longer been the wide rich open spaces into which Americans could retreat and start a new life. During our generation, therefore, the cycle of booms and crashes, which mean mass unemployment, bankruptcies, and the loss of savings, are no longer looked upon by Americans as acts of God, or of inscrutable economic laws which are beyond human control. When most men find that they must work where they live or beg charity from their neighbors, they will no longer accept the spirit and the principles of laissez-faire. They will not listen to those who still seek to deny that there is a public responsibility to maintain an equilibrium in the economy of the nation. The West is no longer open, and men who have the vote are bound to use it, to compel the government to deal with problems that as private persons they can no longer deal with.

In our time, then, the consequences of unemployment and of economic dislocation have become a recognized national responsibility. The general name for it is Social Security. The prevention of mass unemployment and the regulation of the business cycle are now recognized, except by a disappearing minority, as questions of public policy. The system of free enterprise is therefore no longer what it once was. There is now imposed upon it the obligation to provide reasonably full employment under acceptable conditions of work. This obligation will be enforced by the government, and enterprise is free in so far as it meets the new conditions of its freedom.

2. *The Twentieth-Century Debate*

The great debates of our generation have, in the last analysis, been between those who denied and those who affirmed the need for positive measures to defend the Republic, to maintain foreign intercourse, and to conserve and promote internal order and well-being.

The details of the debates have been confusing. But in retrospect we can now see that the underlying issue in foreign affairs was whether we could still take for granted our long immunity and effortless security. Those who thought we could appeared as pacifists or as isolationists: they did not like armaments, or they did not believe in strategic defenses, or they opposed alliances, or they would not enter an organized association with other nations. Those who thought our immunity was over advocated military preparedness, or the League of Nations, or partnerships and alliances with friendly powers. Among them, as among their pacifist or isolationist opponents, there was much disagreement.

This basic issue has now been settled; there are no responsible voices left to say, as there were a few years ago, that no positive measures of any kind, not even fortifying our outposts, are necessary or desirable. Instead of debating the need for any positive policy, we have now to deliberate upon what kind of positive policy we need.

It is certain that isolationism and laissez-faire belong to the past, and that the debate, which has consumed so large a part of our best intellectual energies for more than forty years, is nearly concluded. In the end the verdict is sure to be that the security and prosperity and welfare of the United States cannot be left to chance, that the fundamental issues of national existence have now to be dealt with consciously and positively.

3. The New Age

This will bring about a deep transformation of our political culture. The working habits of American public life were formed in the nineteenth century — broadly speaking in the age which extended from Jackson to McKinley. In the history of the world this period is known as the Victorian Age. With Jackson the direction of American affairs was no longer in the hands of the Founding Fathers, that is to say with the men who over a period of half a century dealt with the fundamental issues of national existence. With McKinley there began the age in which we live: it opened with the conquest of the Philippines which extended American commitments to the coasts of Asia, and ever since it has been increasingly evident that the controlling conditions of our life have changed.

American political slogans of the twentieth century have acknowledged this change. President Franklin Roosevelt proclaimed the advent of a *New* Deal. His predecessor, President Hoover, proclaimed a *New* Era. President Wilson proclaimed a *New* Freedom. Theodore Roosevelt as a candidate for a third term in 1912 proclaimed a *New* Nationalism. The newness in all of them — their least common denominator so to speak — was an awareness that a radical change in the American environment called for new measures, and, therefore, a deliberate formation of public policy.

But the habits of nearly a century were not easily changed. It has proved to be an exceedingly difficult thing for the American people to agree on the formation of policy. It would have been easier if they had had only to alter their public policies. But in fact they are having to form policy where none has existed. For isolationism and laissez-faire individualism are not policies. Their charm, which gives those of us who were reared in the Age of Innocence a nostalgic affection for them, was that they were not policies. They exempted men from public thought and public effort. To be able to say that we need *not* be involved in the affairs of other nations and that the best government is the one which governs *least* was to say that there were no great public issues. It followed that the burdens and duties of the citizen were extremely light.

The leaders of the American people, and the teachers of American youth, have until recently been men educated in the nineteenth century. They come from an age when politics were a diversion and when there was no urgent need to know the art of forming public policy. Now suddenly we find ourselves in enormously difficult times. We have had to make momentous decisions of policy before we had completely rediscovered, much less mastered, the art of forming public policy. The wars, the economic and social disorders, showed that policy had to be formed. The country had the military and economic power to carry out policies when they were formed. But we are a generation who have lacked the skill and self-confidence — the know-how — and this we are having to acquire painfully by trial and error.

Not since the Civil War have the American people had to call on the statesmanship which the Founding Fathers possessed in such an extraordinary degree. During the nineteenth century the naval supremacy of Great Britain maintained an international order within which there were no great wars of aggression. The commercial and financial supremacy of Great Britain maintained an economic order within which an ample supply of European capital was to be had for the development of this country.

At the turn of the century the end of the Victorian order was indicated — by the rising German and Japanese naval power, the decline of British commercial supremacy relative to the new industrial power of the United States, Germany, and Japan. The First World War destroyed the foundations of the Victorian order. Great Britain was no longer strong enough to sustain its system of security, and London, no longer the leading creditor, alone could not manage the commercial system. In the interlude between the two World Wars no viable substitute for the Victorian order was established. For lack of an order which made life secure and tolerable, mankind sat hypnotized like a chicken bewitched by a snake, and saw with fascinated horror that it was drifting inexorably through anarchy to a second World War.

Here at home the effortless security of the decades after the Civil War left a deep impress upon the customs of our people and the character of our public life. It permitted an unconcern with public responsibilities; each individual could concentrate on his own private career. The primary virtues, almost the exclusive virtues, were held to be self-reliance, private initiative, private prudence, and private effort. Unthreatened from abroad, living in a prosperous world economy for which others were responsible, and with opportunity at home abundant and varied, public duty shrank to a very small place in the interests of most men. Public life became the special province of professional politicians and of professional reformers. The ablest men rarely ventured to set foot within it. Private business was the predominant interest of the people. Public affairs were an outlying province, eccentric to the chief concern of American life.

The exceptionally private character of American life has been reflected in American education. The humanistic studies are the traditional discipline in which Western public men, not least among them the founders of the Republic,[1] have been trained. No other discipline is known for the education of statesmen. But in the second half of the nineteenth century this discipline was supplanted in American schools and colleges by curricula avowedly designed either as vocational training for private careers or as a schooling in social reform.

[1] Cf. James J. Walsh, *Education of the Founding Fathers of the Republic*, Fordham University Press, New York, 1935.

Now that the nation must again face the great public issues, we feel the effects: we find that the graduates of our schools are men who have been trained for private careers, or for rather specialized reforms. Hence the contemporary quarrel between the conservatives and the intellectuals, the businessmen and the professors. They do not speak the same language because they are separated from the common intellectual discipline and humanist tradition of Western civilization.

American institutions were established by men who because they were imbued with the great tradition knew what were the great questions of public life. During the long period of immunity and innocence this tradition was all but lost: it came to be regarded as "academic." Thus in our public life we fell into political habits which made it inordinately difficult for the nation to form public policy. Politics became an arena in which local and private interests competed and compromised their conflicts. The very idea of representative government, that is to say of government by men who represented the nation and its enduring interests and significance, gave way to government by delegates.

The Executive, accountable to a larger constituency than any individual Congressman or Senator, has therefore become the focus of the national interest and purpose. For at worst a President does at least represent an agglomeration, or the algebraic sum, of the pressures of many private, local interests. At best he represents the nation above and beyond its constituent parts. So all

Presidents must eventually quarrel with their legislatures, and sooner or later they all do.

This was not the promise of American institutions. The condition is constantly deplored. Yet it has not come about, as our enemies and unfriendly critics say, because of the moral degeneracy of our people. It has come about because public life in the United States has been dormant for nearly a century, and private life has been intense and all-absorbing. The rewards of a private career have been tremendous; since the Civil War the issues of public life have been so secondary that Americans have not had to take seriously the public life of a citizen. The duties of the citizen came to seem very nearly irrelevant to the career of the individual.

American political life has, therefore, become privately centered and introverted. In the years of peace the professional politicians confronted one another on issues which interested the particular constituency to which each of them owed his election. The exceptions are conspicuous men; even in wartime the debates in Congress are conducted with little concern for, often with no consciousness of, the effect of what is said upon our allies, our enemies, or even upon our own armed forces.

These habits and attitudes come down to us from the epoch after the Civil War when politics was an enclosed system, insulated from the main concerns of the people and from all great issues upon which depends the life of the nation. The triviality of debate, and its irresponsibility, are the aftermath of a long age in which, as a matter of fact, public men did not have to deal with great issues. The legislature is introverted. For want of practice, and of urgent need, it has not the habit of deliberation by which high policy can be formed.

In the long period of immunity and of effortless security, the executive branch of the government did not develop the organs for determining and administering high policy. Even when, as has been the case with Theodore Roosevelt, Wilson, Hoover, and Franklin D. Roosevelt, the President has been well aware that the nineteenth century and the American Age of Innocence were over, he has not had a government equipped to make effective what he had perceived was necessary. National policies cannot be formulated without reliable information: even at the outbreak of the Second World War it may be said, without exaggeration or injustice, that the United States government had no effective military, political, and intelligence service. Information, when it is available, has to be elucidated and assessed, and plans of action formulated in accord with it.[2] This is the function of a staff. In 1941 the executive branch of the government had to begin to improvise the procedure for formulating policy which made coherent its diplomacy, its strategy, its industrial mobilization, the civilian requirements, its foreign economic relations and its propaganda.

[2] For a penetrating critique of the Department of State, see Joseph M. Jones, *A Modern Foreign Policy for the United States*. The Macmillan Company, New York, 1944.

The organs which form policy are lacking because they were not needed in the nineteenth century. They are being developed now that we do need them. But it is not easy for elderly men to acquire new habits late in life. It is not easy for the younger men who were trained by the elderly men to do successfully and quickly things they never expected to have to do. Our minds and our political habits lag behind our needs. For they are about a generation behind the times. This is what causes our troubles, and when we groan about "Washington" this is what we are complaining about.

But the things we complain about today are the results not of the attempt to do great things and of failing, but of a long habit of not having to do the great things. Trivial, unimportant issues do not evoke the noble spirit of any people. It is when they are profoundly challenged that they exert themselves fully and believe in their destiny.

The American people are challenged as they have never been before. They are exerting themselves more fully than they have done before. If they can see their duty, they will embrace it, not reluctantly but gladly, because it will restore to their personal lives a meaning they sorely miss, and to being an American the luster and the splendor of an imperishable idea.

4. The American Destiny

Fate has brought it about that America is at the center, no longer on the edges, of Western civilization.

In this fact resides the American destiny. We can deny the fact and refuse our destiny. If we do, Western civilization, which is the glory of our world, will become a disorganized and decaying fringe around the Soviet Union and the emergent peoples of Asia. But if we comprehend our destiny we shall become equal to it. The vision is there, and our people need not perish.

For America is now called to do what the founders and the pioneers always believed was the American task: to make the New World a place where the ancient faith can flourish anew, and its eternal promise at last be redeemed. To ask whether the American nation will rise to this occasion and be equal to its destiny is to ask whether Americans have the will to live. We need have no morbid doubts about that.

The American idea is not an eccentricity in the history of mankind. It is a hope and a pledge of fulfillment. The American idea is founded upon an image of man and of his place in the universe, of his reason and his will, his knowledge of good and evil, his hope of a higher and a natural law which is above all governments, and indeed of all particular laws: this tradition descends to Americans, as to all the Westerners, from the Mediterranean world of the ancient Greeks, Hebrews, and Romans. The Atlantic is now the mediterranean sea of this culture and this faith.

It is no accident — it is indeed historic and providential — that the formation of the first universal order since classical times should begin with the binding together of the dismembered parts of Western Christendom. From this beginning a great prospect offers itself: that the schism between East and West, which opened up in the Dark Ages from the fifth to the eleventh centuries of our era, may at last be healed.

This, I believe, is the prophecy which events announce. Whether we now hear it gladly or shrink away from it suspiciously, it will yet come to pass.

WILSON'S FOURTEEN POINTS

I. Open covenants of peace, openly arrived at, after which there shall be no private international understandings of any kind but diplomacy shall proceed always frankly and in the public view.

II. Absolute freedom of navigation upon the seas, outside territorial waters, alike in peace and in war, except as the seas may be closed in whole or in part by international action for the enforcement of international covenants.

III. The removal, so far as possible, of all economic barriers and the establishment of an equality of trade conditions among all the nations consenting to the peace and associating themselves for its maintenance.

IV. Adequate guarantees given and taken that national armaments will be reduced to the lowest point consistent with domestic safety.

V. A free, open-minded, and absolutely impartial adjustment of all colonial claims, based upon a strict observance of the principle that in determining all such questions of sovereignty the interests of the populations concerned must have equal weight with the equitable claims of the government whose title is to be determined.

VI. The evacuation of all Russian territory and such a settlement of all questions affecting Russia as will secure the best and freest co-operation of the other nations of the world in obtaining for her an unhampered and unembarrassed opportunity for the independent determination of her own political development and national policy and assure her of a sincere welcome into the society of free nations under institutions of her own choosing; and, more than a welcome, assistance also of every kind that she may need and may herself desire. The treatment accorded Russia by her sister nations in the months to come will be the acid test of their good will, of their comprehension of her needs as distinguished from their own interests, and of their intelligent and unselfish sympathy.

VII. Belgium, the whole world will agree, must be evacuated and restored, without any attempt to limit the sovereignty which she enjoys in common with all other free nations. No other single act will serve as this will serve to restore confidence among the nations in the laws which they have themselves set and determined for the government of their relations with one another. Without this healing act the whole structure and validity of international law is forever impaired.

VIII. All French territory should be freed and the invaded portions restored, and the wrong done to France by Prussia in 1871 in the matter of Alsace-Lorraine, which has unsettled the peace of the world for nearly fifty years, should be righted, in order that peace may once more be made secure in the interest of all.

IX. A readjustment of the frontiers of Italy should be effected along clearly recognizable lines of nationality.

X. The peoples of Austria-Hungary, whose place among the nations we wish to see safeguarded and assured, should be accorded the freest opportunity of autonomous development.

XI. Rumania, Serbia, and Montenegro should be evacuated; occupied territories restored; Serbia accorded free and secure access to the sea; and the relations of the several Balkan states to one another determined by friendly counsel along historically established lines of allegiance and nationality; and international guarantees of the political and economic independence and territorial integrity of the several Balkan states should be entered into.

XII. The Turkish portions of the present Ottoman Empire should be assured a secure sovereignty, but the other nationalities which are now under Turkish rule should be assured an undoubted security of life and an absolutely unmolested opportunity of autonomous development, and the Dardanelles should be permanently opened as a free passage to the ships and commerce of all nations under international guarantees.

XIII. An independent Polish state should be erected which should include the territories inhabited by indisputably Polish populations, which should be assured a free and secure access to the sea, and whose political and economic independence and territorial integrity should be guaranteed by international covenant.

XIV. A general association of nations must be formed under specific covenants for the purpose of affording mutual guarantees of political independence and territorial integrity to great and small states alike.

(Woodrow Wilson, January 8, 1918)

WILSON'S FOUR PRINCIPLES

First, that each part of the final settlement *must* be based upon the essential justice of that particular case and upon such adjustments as are most likely to bring a peace that will be permanent;

Second, that peoples and provinces *are not* to be bartered about from sovereignty to sovereignty as if they were mere chattels and pawns in a game, even the great game, now forever discredited, of the balance of power; but that

Third, every territorial settlement involved in this war *must* be made in the interest and for the benefit of the populations concerned, and not as a part of any mere adjustment or compromise of claims amongst rival States; and

Fourth, that all well defined national aspirations *shall be* accorded the utmost satisfaction that can be accorded them without introducing new or perpetuating old elements of discord and antagonism that would be likely in time to break the peace of Europe and consequently of the world.

(Woodrow Wilson, February 11, 1918)

WILSON'S FOUR ENDS

I. The destruction of every arbitrary power anywhere that can separately, secretly, and of its single choice disturb the peace of the world; or, if it cannot be presently destroyed, at the least its reduction to virtual impotence.

II. The settlement of every question, whether of territory, of sovereignty, of economic arrangement, or of political relationship, upon the basis of the free acceptance of that settlement by the people immediately concerned, and not upon the basis of the material interest or advantage of any other nation or people which may desire a different settlement for the sake of its own exterior influence or mastery.

III. The consent of all nations to be governed in their conduct toward each other by the same principles of honor and of respect for the common law of civilized society that govern the individual citizens of all modern States in their relations with one another; to the end that all promises and covenants may be sacredly observed, no private plots or conspiracies hatched, no selfish injuries wrought with impunity, and a mutual trust established upon the handsome foundation of a mutual respect for right.

IV. The establishment of an organization of peace which shall make it certain that the combined power of free nations will check every invasion of right and serve to make peace and justice the more secure by affording a definite tribunal of opinion to which all must submit and by which every international readjustment that cannot be amicably agreed upon by the peoples directly concerned shall be sanctioned.

(Woodrow Wilson, July 4, 1918)

WILSON'S FIVE PARTICULARS

First, the impartial justice meted out must involve no discrimination between those to whom we wish to be just and those to whom we do not wish to be just. It must be a justice that plays no favorites and knows no standard but the equal rights of the several peoples concerned;

Second, no special or separate interest of any single nation or any group of nations can be made the basis of any part of the settlement which is not consistent with the common interest of all;

Third, there can be no leagues or alliances or special covenants and understandings within the general and common family of the League of Nations;

Fourth, and more specifically, there can be no special, selfish economic combinations within the league and no employment or any form of economic boycott or exclusion except as the power of economic penalty by exclusion from the markets of the world may be vested in the League of Nations itself as a means of discipline and control;

Fifth, all international agreements and treaties of every kind must be made known in their entirety to the rest of the world.

(Woodrow Wilson, September 27, 1918)

DECLARATION OF PRINCIPLES, KNOWN AS THE ATLANTIC CHARTER, BY THE PRESIDENT OF THE UNITED STATES OF AMERICA AND THE PRIME MINISTER OF THE UNITED KINGDOM, AUGUST 14, 1941

The President of the United States of America and the Prime Minister, Mr. Churchill, representing His Majesty's Government in the United Kingdom, being met together, deem it right to make known certain common principles in the national policies of their respective countries on which they base their hopes for a better future for the world.

First, their countries seek no aggrandizement, territorial or other;

Second, they desire to see no territorial changes that do not accord with the freely expressed wishes of the peoples concerned;

Third, they respect the right of all peoples to choose the form of government under which they will live; and they wish to see sovereign rights and self-government restored to those who have been forcibly deprived of them;

Fourth, they will endeavor, with due respect for their existing obligations, to further the enjoyment by all States, great or small, victor or vanquished, of access, on equal terms, to the trade and to the raw materials of the world which are needed for their economic prosperity;

Fifth, they desire to bring about the fullest collaboration between all nations in the economic field with the object of securing, for all, improved labor standards, economic advancement and social security;

Sixth, after the final destruction of the Nazi tyranny, they hope to see established a peace which will afford to all nations the means of dwelling in safety within their own boundaries, and which will afford assurance that all the men in all the lands may live out their lives in freedom from fear and want;

Seventh, such a peace should enable all men to traverse the high seas and oceans without hindrance;

Eighth, they believe that all of the nations of the world, for realistic as well as spiritual reasons must come to the abandonment of the use of force. Since no future peace can be maintained if land, sea or air armaments continue to be employed by nations which threaten, or may threaten, aggression outside of their frontiers, they believe, pending the establishment of a wider and permanent system of general security, that the disarmament of such nations is essential. They will likewise aid and encourage all other practicable measures which will lighten for peace-loving peoples the crushing burden of armaments.

DECLARATION BY UNITED NATIONS:

A JOINT DECLARATION BY THE UNITED STATES OF AMERICA, THE UNITED KINGDOM OF GREAT BRITAIN AND NORTHERN IRELAND, THE UNION OF SOVIET SOCIALIST REPUBLICS, CHINA, AUSTRALIA, BELGIUM, CANADA, COSTA RICA, CUBA, CZECHOSLOVAKIA, DOMINICAN REPUBLIC, EL SALVADOR, GREECE, GUATEMALA, HAITI, HONDURAS, INDIA, LUXEMBOURG, NETHERLANDS, NEW ZEALAND, NICARAGUA, NORWAY, PANAMA, POLAND, SOUTH AFRICA, YUGOSLAVIA.

The Governments signatory hereto,

Having subscribed to a common program of purposes and principles embodied in the Joint Declaration of the President of the United States of America and the Prime Minister of the United Kingdom of Great Britain and Northern Ireland dated August 14, 1941, known as the Atlantic Charter.

Being convinced that complete victory over their enemies is essential to defend life, liberty, independence and religious freedom, and to preserve human rights and justice in their own lands as well as in other lands, and that they are now engaged in a common struggle against savage and brutal forces seeking to subjugate the world, DECLARE:

(1) Each Government pledges itself to employ its full resources, military or economic, against those members of the Tripartite Pact and its adherents with which such government is at war.

(2) Each Government pledges itself to co-operate with the Governments signatory hereto and not to make a separate armistice or peace with the enemies.

The foregoing declaration may be adhered to by other nations which are, or which may be, rendering material assistance and contributions in the struggle for victory over Hitlerism.

Done at Washington
January First, 1942

DECLARATION OF FOUR NATIONS ON GENERAL SECURITY

The Governments of the United States of America, the United Kingdom, the Soviet Union and China:

united in their determination, in accordance with the Declaration by the United Nations of January 1, 1942, and subsequent declarations, to continue hostilities against those Axis powers with which they respectively are at war until such powers have laid down their arms on the basis of unconditional surrender;

conscious of their responsibility to secure the liberation of themselves and the peoples allied with them from the menace of aggression;

recognizing the necessity of ensuring a rapid and orderly transition from war to peace and of establishing and maintaining international peace and security with the least diversion of the world's human and economic resources for armaments;

jointly declare:

1. That their united action, pledged for the prosecution of the war against their respective enemies, will be continued for the organization and maintenance of peace and security.

2. That those of them at war with a common enemy will act together in all matters relating to the surrender and disarmament of that enemy.

3. That they will take all measures deemed by them to be necessary to provide against any violation of the terms imposed upon the enemy.

4. That they recognize the necessity of establishing at

the earliest practicable date a general international organization, based on the principle of the sovereign equality of all peace-loving states, and open to membership by all such states, large and small, for the maintenance of international peace and security.

5. That for the purpose of maintaining international peace and security pending the re-establishment of law and order and the inauguration of a system of general security, they will consult with one another and as occasion requires with other members of the United Nations with a view to joint action on behalf of the community of nations.

6. That after the termination of hostilities they will not employ their military forces within the territories of other states except for the purposes envisaged in this declaration and after joint consultation.

7. That they will confer and co-operate with one another and with other members of the United Nations to bring about a practicable general agreement with respect to the regulation of armaments in the post-war period.

Moscow,
  30th October, 1943.

V. MOLOTOV
ANTHONY EDEN
CORDELL HULL
FOO PING-SHEUNG

DECLARATION REGARDING ITALY

The Foreign Secretaries of the United States of America, the United Kingdom and the Soviet Union have established that their three Governments are in complete agreement that Allied policy towards Italy must be based upon the fundamental principle that Fascism and all its evil influences and emanations shall be utterly destroyed and that the Italian people shall be given every opportunity to establish governmental and other institutions based upon democratic principles.

The Foreign Secretaries of the United States of America and the United Kingdom declare that the action of their Governments from the inception of the invasion of Italian territory, in so far as paramount military requirements have permitted, has been based upon this policy.

In the furtherance of this policy in the future the Foreign Secretaries of the three Governments are agreed that the following measures are important and should be put into effect:

1. It is essential that the Italian Government should be made more democratic by the introduction of representatives of those sections of the Italian people who have always opposed Fascism.

2. Freedom of speech, of religious worship, of political belief, of the press and of public meeting shall be restored in full measure to the Italian people, who shall also be entitled to form anti-Fascist political groups.

3. All institutions and organizations created by the Fascist regime shall be suppressed.

4. All Fascist or pro-Fascist elements shall be removed from the administration and from the institutions and organizations of a public character.

5. All political prisoners of the Fascist regime shall be released and accorded a full amnesty.

6. Democratic organs of local government shall be created.

7. Fascist chiefs and other persons known or suspected to be war criminals shall be arrested and handed over to justice.

In making this declaration the three Foreign Secretaries recognize that so long as active military operations continue in Italy the time at which it is possible to give full effect to the principles set out above will be determined by the Commander-in-Chief on the basis of instructions received through the Combined Chiefs of Staff. The three Governments parties to this declaration will at the request of any one of them consult on this matter.

It is further understood that nothing in this resolution is to operate against the right of the Italian people ultimately to choose their own form of government.

(Moscow, October 30, 1943)

DECLARATION OF THE THREE POWERS

We — The President of the United States, the Prime Minister of Great Britain, and the Premier of the Soviet Union, have met these four days past, in this, the Capital of our Ally, Iran, and have shaped and confirmed our common policy.

We express our determination that our nations shall work together in war and in the peace that will follow.

As to war — our military staffs have joined in our round table discussions, and we have concerted our plans for the destruction of the German forces. We have reached complete agreement as to the scope and timing of the operations to be undertaken from the east, west and south.

The common understanding which we have here reached guarantees that victory will be ours.

And as to peace — we are sure that our concord will win an enduring Peace. We recognize fully the supreme responsibility resting upon us and all the United Nations to make a peace which will command the goodwill of the overwhelming mass of the peoples of the world and banish the scourge and terror of war for many generations.

With our Diplomatic advisors we have surveyed the problems of the future. We shall seek the co-operation and active participation of all nations, large and small, whose peoples in heart and mind are dedicated, as are our own peoples, to the elimination of tyranny and slavery, oppression and intolerance. We will welcome them, as they may choose to come, into a world family of Democratic Nations.

No power on earth can prevent our destroying the German armies by land, their U Boats by sea, and their war plants from the air.

Our attack will be relentless and increasing.

Emerging from these cordial conferences we look with confidence to the day when all peoples of the world may live free lives, untouched by tyranny, and according to their varying desires and their own consciences.

We came here with hope and determination. We leave here, friends in fact, in spirit and in purpose.

ROOSEVELT, CHURCHILL AND STALIN

Signed at Teheran, December 1, 1943

APPENDIX X

CAIRO STATEMENT ON JAPAN

The several military missions have agreed upon future military operations against Japan. The Three Great Allies expressed their resolve to bring unrelenting pressure against their brutal enemies by sea, land, and air. This pressure is already rising.

The Three Great Allies are fighting this war to restrain and punish the aggression of Japan. They covet no gain for themselves and have no thought of territorial expansion. It is their purpose that Japan shall be stripped of all the islands in the Pacific which she has seized or occupied since the beginning of the first World War in 1914, and that all the territories Japan has stolen from the Chinese, such as Manchuria, Formosa, and the Pescadores, shall be restored to the Republic of China. Japan will also be expelled from all other territories which she has taken by violence and greed. The aforesaid three great powers, mindful of the enslavement of the people of Korea, are determined that in due course Korea shall become free and independent.

With these objects in view the three Allies, in harmony with those of the United Nations at war with Japan, will continue to persevere in the serious and prolonged operations necessary to procure the unconditional surrender of Japan.

(December 1, 1943)

HULL'S SEVENTEEN POINTS

Our Fundamental National Interests

In determining our foreign policy we must first see clearly what our true national interests are.

At the present time, the paramount aim of our foreign policy is to defeat our enemies as quickly as possible.

Beyond final victory, our fundamental national interests are the assuring of our national security and the fostering of the economic and social well-being of our people.

International Co-operation

Co-operation between nations in the spirit of good neighbors, founded on the principles of liberty, equality, justice, morality, and law, is the most effective method of safeguarding and promoting the political, the economic, the social, and the cultural well-being of our nation and of all nations.

International Organization Backed by Force

Some international agency must be created which can — by force, if necessary — keep the peace among nations in the future.

A system of organized international co-operation for the maintenance of peace must be based upon the willingness of the co-operating nations to use force, if necessary, to keep the peace. There must be certainty that adequate and appropriate means are available and will be used for this purpose.

Political Differences

Political differences which present a threat to the peace of the world should be submitted to agencies which would use the remedies of discussion, negotiation, conciliation, and good offices.

International Court of Justice

Disputes of a legal character which present a threat to the peace of the world should be adjudicated by an international court of justice whose decisions would be based upon application of principles of law.

Reduction of Arms

International co-operative action must include eventual adjustment of national armaments in such a manner that the rule of law cannot be successfully challenged and that the burden of armaments may be reduced to a minimum.

Moscow Four-Nation Declaration

Through this declaration the Soviet Union, Great Britain, the United States, and China have laid the foundation for co-operative effort in the post-war world toward enabling all peace-loving nations, large and small, to live in peace and security, to preserve the liberties and rights of civilized existence, and to enjoy expanded opportunities and facilities for economic, social, and spiritual progress.

Spheres of Influence and Alliances

As the provisions of the four-nation declaration are carried into effect, there will no longer be need for spheres of influence, for alliances, for balance of power, or any other of the special arrangements through which, in the unhappy past, the nations strove to safeguard their security or to promote their interests.

Surveillance over Aggressor Nations

In the process of re-establishing international order, the United Nations must exercise surveillance over aggressor nations until such time as the latter demonstrate their willingness and ability to live at peace with other nations. How long such surveillance will need to continue must depend upon the rapidity with which the peoples of Germany, Japan, Italy, and their satellites give convincing proof that they have repudiated and abandoned the monstrous philosophy of superior race and conquest by force and have embraced loyally the basic principles of peaceful processes.

International Trade Barriers

Excessive trade barriers of the many different kinds must be reduced, and practices which impose injuries on others and divert trade from its natural economic course must be avoided.

International Finance

Equally plain is the need for making national currencies once more freely exchangeable for each other at stable rates of exchange; for a system of financial relations so devised that materials can be produced and ways may be found of moving them where there are markets created by human need; for machinery through which capital may — for the development of the world's resources and for the stabilization of economic activity — move on equitable terms from financially stronger to financially weaker countries.

Atlantic Charter: Reciprocal Obligations

The pledge of the Atlantic Charter is of a system which will give every nation, large or small, a greater assurance of stable peace, greater opportunity for the realization of its aspirations to freedom, and greater facilities for material advancement. But that pledge implies an obligation for each nation to demonstrate its capacity for stable and progressive government, to fulfil scrupulously its established duties to other nations, to settle its international differences and disputes by none but peaceful methods, and to make its full contribution to the maintenance of enduring peace.

Sovereign Equality of Nations

Each sovereign nation, large or small, is in law and under law the equal of every other nation.

The principle of sovereign equality of all peace-loving states, irrespective of size and strength, as partners in a future system of general security, will be the foundation-stone upon which the future international organization will be constructed.

Form of Government

Each nation should be free to decide for itself the forms and details of its governmental organization — so long as it conducts its affairs in such a way as not to menace the peace and security of other nations.

Non-Intervention

All nations, large and small, which respect the rights of others are entitled to freedom from outside interference in their internal affairs.

Liberty

There is no surer way for men and for nations to show themselves worthy of liberty than to fight for its preservation, in any way that is open to them, against those who would destroy it for all. Never did a plainer duty to fight against its foes devolve upon all peoples who prize liberty and all who aspire to it.

All peoples who, with "a decent respect to the opinions of mankind," have qualified themselves to assume and to discharge the responsibilities of liberty are entitled to its enjoyment.

Dependent Peoples

There rests upon the independent nations a responsibility in relation to dependent peoples who aspire to liberty. It should be the duty of nations having political ties with such peoples, of mandatories, of trustees, or of other agencies, as the case may be, to help the aspiring peoples to develop materially and educationally, to prepare themselves for the duties and responsibilities of self-government, and to attain liberty. An excellent example of what can be achieved is afforded in the record of our relationship with the Philippines.

(March 21, 1944)

SWISS DECREES PROHIBITING EXTREMIST PARTIES

Decree of the Federal Council concerning the dissolution of the "Rassemblement Fédéral" and of the "Nationale Gemeinschaft Schaffhausen"

(of July 6, 1943)

The Swiss Federal Council,
Pursuant to article 3 of the Federal Decree of August 30, 1939 about proper measures to insure the security of the country and the maintenance of its neutrality,

decrees:

Article 1

The "Rassemblement Fédéral" and the "Nationale Gemeinschaft Schaffhausen" are dissolved; every sort of activity is forbidden to them. The newspapers *Die Front* and *Der Grenzbote* are forbidden.

The prohibition includes also the organizations and the newspapers which might be substituted for them.

The members of the "Rassemblement Fédéral" and of the "Nationale Gemeinschaft Schaffhausen," or of organizations which might be substituted for them, cannot be members of a federal, cantonal or communal authority.

Article 2

Violations of the present decree will be punished according to the article of the Federal Council of June 1, 1943 repressing violations of the interdictions of parties.

Article 3

Violations of the present decree are within the competence of the federal jurisdiction.

The Department of Justice and Police can delegate the examination and the judgment to the Cantonal Authorities.

Article 4

The decree of the Federal Council of December 17, 1940 insuring the execution of the one of November 26, 1940 which concerns the dissolution of the communist Swiss party is applicable by analogy.

Article 5

The present decree becomes effective on July 6, 1943.

Bern, July 6, 1943.

In the name of the Swiss Federal Council:
The President of the Confederation, CELIO
The Chancellor of the Confederation, G. BOVET

Decree of the Federal Council concerning the dissolution of the Swiss Communist Party

(of November 26, 1940)

The Swiss Federal Council,

Pursuant to article 102, paragraph 9 and 10 of the Constitution;

Pursuant to article 3 of the Federal Decree of August 30, 1939 on proper measures to insure the security of the country and the maintenance of its neutrality,

decrees:

Article 1

All communist organizations existing in Switzerland are dissolved; any kind of activity is forbidden to them. The prohibition includes also the groups which might be substituted for the dissolved organizations.

Communists cannot be members of any Federal, Cantonal or Communal authority.

Article 2

Are reserved the dispositions of the Federal Council of August 6, 1940 establishing measures against communist or anarchist activity. The infringements of the article one of the present decree will be prosecuted according to article two of the aforementioned decree.

Article 3

The present decree becomes effective on November 27, 1940.

Berne, November 26, 1940

> In the name of the Swiss Federal Council:
> The President of the Confederation
> PILET-GOLAZ
> The Chancellor of the Confederation
> G. BOVET